conformed, reborn, transformed

a spiritual journey

lance mosher

Conformed, Reborn, Transformed: A Spiritual Journey

First Print Edition: August 2013

Printed in the United States of America

ISBN: 978-0-9897041-0-6

www.conformedreborntransformed.com

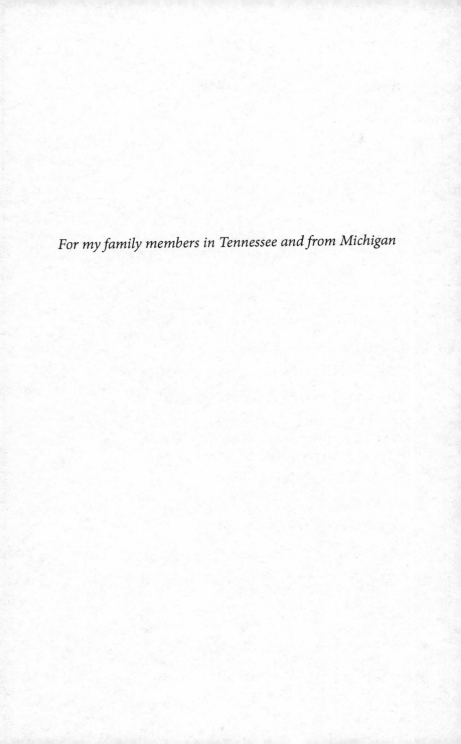

For my family members in Tennessee and from Michigan

Foreword

If I had to pick one word that best describes Lance, it would be "dedicated." In all aspects of his life he has always shown great dedication: dedication toward his school work, toward his friends, toward his music, toward his job. Even when we flipped burgers together in Henderson, TN, he put everything he had into the job. It wasn't because the money was so great (we made minimum wage), or because advancement was so competitive. Lance just always put his heart into everything he did.

So it should have come as no surprise when he became so dedicated to God after obeying the gospel. I've seen a number of new Christians come up from the waters of baptism, hug their friends and family, and then take their place on the pew every Sunday as just another name on the roster. But Lance recognized the seriousness of sin in the world and the consequences that others faced because of it and decided to do something about it.

Long before deciding to do mission work, he was constantly bringing friends over to our weekly Bible studies to teach them about God's plan of salvation. He was a new Christian and didn't know the Scriptures very well yet, so he led his friends to others who did. Many souls can now look forward to hearing the blessed Savior tell them one day, "Well done, good and faithful servant" (Matthew 25:21), because of the dedication Lance has shown to God and his great commission to "Go into all the world and proclaim the gospel to the whole creation" (Mark 16:15).

Conformed, Reborn, Transformed is a journey through the spiritual experiences that Lance had from an early childhood up through finding and obeying Christ. Throughout this journey, he encounters different faiths, different interpretations of God's word, and different attitudes toward sin and salvation.

Reading this book struck me on a personal level because Lance's journey through faith very much mirrored my own. Other than the specific denominations that he encountered, he and I had almost identical experiences in regard to what we were taught about salvation, when we believed we were saved, doubts about our salvation, and finally, meeting someone who actually sat down and spent time going through God's word with us until we came to see the simple truth within its pages. We did not believe it because someone told us it was true, but because we finally saw it for ourselves. It gives me hope that if this process worked for us, it will work for others who are in the same position in which we both once were.

Conformed, Reborn, Transformed is especially relevant in today's denominational world where the idea of "I'm okay; you're okay" has run rampant. So many lost souls have no idea that they are lost, because they've given into this idea that finding a church is about what pleases you, not what pleases the Lord. So many people's faith is based on what they've been told and taught by others rather than what is in the word of God. "My people are destroyed for lack of knowledge" (Hosea 4:6).

Lance discovered some difficult truths and made some hard decisions in his life to get to where he is today, as he describes in this book. Friends, family, and people whom he looked up to and respected greatly had all taught him things that were contrary to the word of God, and he had to decide with whom he would stand. If it wasn't for his dedication to seeking God and God's truth at all costs, he might have taken the broad way that leads to destruction (Matthew 7:13).

I admire Lance greatly. He is one of my role models for what a true Christian should be, and for how one should conduct oneself to please the Lord. From the time we started studying together, I could tell that he was more interested in finding the truth than defending his current faith. If everyone had this same attitude, then perhaps the narrow way that leads to life (Matthew 7:14) would be a little more crowded. It is evident that this book was written out of love and concern for the souls of others, and I hope you will read it with that in mind. But more than that, I hope this book will help you discover the word of God that is able to eternally save your soul (James 1:21).

Let the word of Christ dwell in you richly... Colossians 3:16.

and you will know the truth, and the truth will set you free. John 8:32.

"DEVIN"
July 2013

Preface

The concept of this book has been rolling through my mind for years. As a man, my life story is not worth sharing. As a man of God, because of what Christ has done for me, I'm convinced that my story must be shared. My friends and family need to know what really happened ten years ago. Strangers will be able to relate to the emotional and intellectual struggles I faced at that time. While exploring the paragraphs, pages, and chapters of this book, readers with able and open minds will wrestle with me, themselves, and even the Lord. Who will win?

In this book, I have done my very best to relate to you the most important events in my life. I know it would be impossible for you to regard them as dear to you as they are to me. I wouldn't want you to, anyway. However, I do hope you enjoy the passage set before you in *Conformed, Reborn, Transformed: A Spiritual Journey*. The story is true. It is my history. Naturally, since the conversations in it took place a decade or more ago, I have had to "fill in the gaps" where memory lacks, but I have done my very best to stay true to what actually happened. While the events indeed took place, and the topics of conversations are accurate, much of the dialogue is posed to best represent the experiences that I am trying to share with you. To protect their rights and privacy, some of the individuals' names of this story have been changed.

Except where otherwise noted, all Scripture quotations in this book are from the English Standard Version (ESV). If you are not familiar with the ESV, please compare the Scripture references to your preferred translation (for example, the King James Version).

I wrote this book to document the most important events in my life. I wrote this book to teach. I wrote this book to show the providence of God. I wrote this book to show Jesus Christ to other people. This is my spiritual autobiography, which means I only tried to reveal those things that are related to my spiritual journey in life. Beware; I didn't hold back.

He must increase, but I must decrease. John 3:30.

I love you with the love of the Lord.

LANCE MOSHER
August 2013

Buffy, Buffet

1989 - 1990; Phoenix, Arizona

My sister and I were in the back seat of a blue sedan. I was on the right side, and she was on the left. That's the way it always was. In those seats, we learned neat facts from our parents, my toys battled it out with each other, and my sister taught me how to tell time. There was one particular road near Phoenix that we loved riding down, because our dad would go a bit faster than normal, and at the pinnacle of the small hills, our stomachs would have a funny feeling in them. "Whoa!" we would exclaim together. I was about four years old, and she was about eight.

On this specific evening in that blue car, it was the first time I ever remembered going to a church function. Our family had gone several times before, but this one scored "earliest spiritual memory."

"What are we gonna do there?" I asked my mother.

"They're putting on a buffet."

That sounded very strange to me. My grandmother had a dog named Buffy, but I had never heard of a buffet before. I wondered how they were related.

Most children ask any and all questions on their mind. I wasn't much different in that regard. However, when an adult would give me a close-ended answer, not inviting me to question further, I would stop. Most other children, however, keep asking, "What? Where? When? How? Why?" I enjoyed figuring things out on my own. I was excited to learn what a buffet had to do with a little brown dog.

When we arrived at the buffet, I looked for a small dog, but I couldn't find one. *Maybe she'll show up later.* The abundance of food without restrictions quickly put the furry pup out of my mind.

I was a picky eater. I probably gave my parents more gray hairs over complaining about food than anything else. "This isn't a restaurant," was my dad's standard reply when I complained about what he put on my plate.

I wonder if this counts as a restaurant, I thought, looking over the rows and rows of food.

The Lutheran Church building had a large painting of a lion in the foyer. That was my favorite thing to look at while at church. Special events like Easter, Christmas, and buffets were the times I went to church with my parents and sister, though my grandparents took me more frequently.

My grandparents seemed to know everyone at church. While waiting on them to finish their coffee and conversations after church, I sometimes tried to open my hearing up to all of the conversations around me at once. The recognizable cacophony was a sensational phenomenon for a young, curious person like me. Sometimes, I would mumble to myself, feeling like I was adding to the disorganized, yet obviously important, verbal symphony.

Growing up, I had a nightly routine with my mother before my bedtime.

"Have you brushed your teeth?"

"Yep!"

"Let me smell," we would play out.

My dad was sometimes there, but my time with my mom before bed made a bigger impact. During our nightly routine, she also taught me my first prayer.

"Now I lay me down to sleep. I pray the Lord my soul to keep. And if I die before I wake, I pray the Lord my soul to take. Amen." I had no idea what I was saying, but I grew up to appreciate so much that my parents took the time to teach me to pray before bed. Sometimes, the routine of brushing my teeth before bed was broken here and there over the years. However, there was not a time growing up when I did not pray before bed, even when my parents were not around. In my little mind, I imagined Jesus in heaven, receiving my prayers and smiling down while sitting among Santa Claus, the Easter Bunny, and the Tooth Fairy.

My parents separated and divorced when I was five years old. Being so young, I didn't understand it. I had so many questions. I remember spending a lot of time with my grandparents during that time, especially my grandmother. My grandmother was so patient with my sister and me. She would spend her time teaching us the lessons of life. One of the most valuable lessons I learned from her was that God can listen to our prayers even when it's not time to eat or go to bed. There was one evening at my grandmother's house that she had her whole family over. As my family would always say, "It was a big time!" As they were all on the back patio, enjoying

3

their time with their booze and each other, my grandmother noticed me by myself. Coming over, she asked, "What's wrong, Lancer?" She always called me "Lancer."

"I want Mom and Dad to get back together."

"Why don't you pray to God that that will happen?" Leaving me to follow her instructions, I wandered to my grandparents' legendarily soft grass, looked up to the nearly full moon, and told God exactly what was on my heart. I wanted so badly for God to bring my parents back together.

Though God did not grant my little heart's prayer, the lesson I learned from my grandmother was vitally important to the rest of my spiritual life.

Northern Journey

1990 - 1995; Rogers City, Michigan

"I want you to meet someone," my father said. Soon after my parents' divorce, my father, having already moved out of the house, brought to my mother's house a woman almost twenty years younger than he was. I didn't fully understand the situation at six years old, but I later learned that she would become my new "mom."

Not long after this initial meeting, my father moved to Michigan (his home state), taking along his new "friend."

Soon after that, leaving our mother behind, my sister and I were with our grandparents and Buffy, the little brown dog, in the cab of a pickup truck. We traveled for four days, spanning the 2,000 plus miles from Phoenix, Arizona, to Rogers City, Michigan. It was the summer after my kindergarten year, and it was my sister's and my first visit to Michigan.

When we arrived at our dad's new house, our home for the summer, we knew that we would all be forced to grow close to each other during those three months. The house didn't even have an official bedroom. Our dad had built makeshift bunk beds for my sister and me in the "mud room" (where you kick off your shoes before going inside). He and the lady, whom he had recently married and that he forced us to refer to as "Mom," slept behind a room divider in the living room. This trip to Michigan began an annual tradition of traveling by plane or car to spend the entire summer in Michigan with our dad's family.

"Our Father which art in heaven, Hallowed be thy name." That is the first bit of Scripture I ever memorized (Matthew 6:9, King James Version). I prayed it on a nightly basis, sitting on the plywood bunk beds with my sister, my father, and his new wife. That summer, my dad taught me to say the "Lord's Prayer" in full. I felt quite proud of myself when I could say it completely without help.

The next summer, my sister and I were quite happy when we arrived, and we learned that our dad had added a second level to the house. That year, we had a real bedroom with real bunk beds!

That summer was the first time I ever learned about the popular Bible stories in Genesis, beyond Adam and Eve. My sister, my cousins, and I enrolled in a Vacation Bible School at the Lutheran Church near my uncle's home in Rogers City. Making crafts from construction paper, glue, and glitter, we learned of Noah, Abraham, and Joseph.

"I want to marry Jesus," I explained to my new step-mom.

"You can't marry Jesus. He's a boy!"

As I learned more and more about Bible stories, I felt I knew more and more about the man who heard my prayers. The more I learned, the more I loved him. I wasn't the only one who acted more interested in God. It seemed that the move to Rogers City revamped my father's family's faith. We were going to church much more regularly than we did in Phoenix.

That summer, while my sister and I were in Michigan, my mother and my maternal aunt, though they had no friends or family in the southern United States, moved to Henderson, Tennessee, on a whim. I remember my sister's devastation when she heard the news that Mom had moved to Tennessee. We would not be going home to Phoenix at the end of the summer. We would be going to a new home. We would never see our friends at school again. We would have to go to a new school and make new friends. I was too young to understand the implications, but based on my sister's reaction, none of it was good news.

Second grade was my first year in Henderson. I attended preschool, kindergarten, and first grade in Phoenix. Starting with my second grade year, apart from my fourth grade year, which I spent in Michigan, I spent every school year in Henderson until I graduated high school.

As the summers went by, I began to understand more and more at Sunday school, and since my mother stopped going to church after the divorce, my time in Michigan was my only opportunity to learn about the Bible. Spiritually speaking, things were progressing for me. I assumed the same was happening with my sister. I am very thankful to my father for showing an interest in our spiritual welfare.

During her eighth grade year, my sister showed more spiritual interest than I had ever seen from her. Since she was old enough, she started catechism classes at the local Lutheran Church. By the end of her study, she was officially "confirmed" in the Lutheran Church. My family told me that since I was also baptized as a baby, I would eventually go through confirmation, too. After seeing the overall reaction my family had to my sister's confirmation, I looked forward to it.

One year, while we were back in Tennessee with our mother, I learned that my father and stepmother had divorced. By the time the next summer came around, he had begun the dating process again and was engaged to the woman who would eventually be our second stepmother. My sister had previously befriended her daughter, so we had already met our father's fiancée. My sister was quite excited to gain her friend as a sister, and I eventually grew very close to her, as well.

Southern Prayer

1995 - 1998; Henderson, Tennessee

Moving to Tennessee on an impulse was an opportunity for my mother and aunt to start life over. After I finally understood what the move meant, it was upsetting to leave my friends in Phoenix behind. However, I was able to make friends in Henderson quite easily.

"I have to meet his mother first," was my mother's response when I asked her in third grade if I could spend the night with my new friend, Derek Thorton.

That week, I retrieved Derek's phone number, so my mother could call his mom. Going to his house for the first time, my mother was able to meet Mrs. Laura and Mr. Michael.

After my mom "approved" Derek and his family, we quickly became inseparable. I was at his house almost every weekend. Since I had spent entire summers away from my mother, it wasn't hard for me to stay at Derek's house so much. It quickly became a weekly routine for me to go to school with a backpack of clothes so that I could easily ride the bus home with Derek, instead of relying on one of the moms for transportation.

Regarding spiritual things, there were two things my

parents tried to teach me: love God; respect God. The only ways they showed me how to love and respect God were to pray repetitious prayers, live a generally good and clean life, and refrain from using God's name in vain. My parents did the best they knew how with what they had.

Though my family had a large "Family Bible" that my mother kept on the living room hutch, I did not own a personal copy of God's word until one day in fifth grade. I was in Mrs. Bard's class, and some men working for the Gideons asked Mrs. Bard if they could give a gift to all the students. She approved, and on that day (October 29, 1996), we all received our very own pocket-size King James Version New Testament with Psalms and Proverbs. What a special gift it was!

During Derek's and my sixth grade year, Derek's family decided to start going to church. Since they did not belong to a local church, they did what seemed to be the most logical thing to do. They started looking for a church to join. I was usually at their home on Sundays, so I gladly tagged along during their "church hopping" adventure.

Yes, I enjoyed the things that I learned in Sunday school in Rogers City, but my interests were also changing as I grew up in Henderson. I, of course, still believed in God and prayed before bed, but most of my interests in fifth grade were invested in video games and TV.

"He's something special." The pastor was pointing at me during fellowship after the sermon.

Though I sat through many different church services with Derek's family, there was one Sunday service that stood out. There we were: three kids on a pew, wanting to be anywhere but at church. Derek's friend, Dalton, had also spent the night, so he came along, too. Dalton was a developing artist, interested only in art and cars. During the sermon, he and Derek were only paying attention to his latest artistic endeavor. I, however, was watching the pastor pace back and forth up front while he delivered his lengthy message. Was I interested in what he was saying? Truthfully, no. I was much more interested in Dalton's colorful creation. However, my mother had taught me respect, and I didn't feel like it would be respectful to the pastor or God by whispering, "Put blue flames coming out of the tailpipe!"

After services, the pastor was sure to find me. It was then that he told Derek's parents what he made of me. Apparently, he had never seen a kid my age so "interested" in a 45-minute long sermon.

After "testing out" several local churches, Derek's family finally decided to join the local Baptist Church in Henderson. Going to church with the Thorton family most Sundays, I quickly became a regular visitor to the middle-school Sunday school class. We didn't know before then how many of our classmates were Baptists. Almost all the popular kids from school were, actually. We weren't among the popular ones, but I thought that being part of this class might get my foot in the door.

"We're going to some youth thing," Derek told me minutes before the final bell on a Friday afternoon. Though we were still officially in class, I had already zipped up my books and strapped on my backpack. It was awkward sitting in a school desk with my backpack on, but it allowed for faster "up and go" when the bell rang, and everyone raced for the good seats on Bus 25.

"Who's *we*?" I asked.

"Me and you are going with the youth group to Jackson tonight."

"Is it a churchy thing or a like a fun thing?"

"I don't know," Derek said, cocking his head, "but Keith made it sound fun!" Keith was the youth pastor at the Baptist Church.

When we arrived at Union University's campus later on that night, we saw they had a huge tent set up on one of the lawns. We clearly were not the only church at the event. There were probably thirty youth groups there. We all found our seats under the tent to see what kind of show they had for us.

After a brief clown act, things got much more serious. The keynote speaker came on stage with a strong message. This guy was trained for situations like this—being down to earth, yet speaking to the heart. He spoke of sin. He spoke of love. He spoke of heaven. He spoke of hell.

Like most everyone, I had always heard the phrases, "Jesus saves," and, "Jesus died for your sins." That message was always given to me as one of those things that was a simple fact to accept.

"Two plus two equals four. Jesus died for your sins."

"Yep! I agree."

That night, however, under that tent with hundreds of other young persons, I heard for the very first time that the phrase, "Jesus saves," is something I was expected to respond to. After his speech, the speaker of the evening offered the first altar call I had ever heard.

"If this message has moved you tonight, and you want a personal relationship with Jesus Christ, come up to the front, and you will be given a chance to invite Jesus into your heart."

Between the two of us, Derek took the first step. Since this was more of his church event than mine, I was hoping he would take initiative. I was quick to follow.

"I'm glad to see you up here, Derek and Lance," Keith said as if he was waiting on us. "Come this way."

I hadn't really gotten to know Keith very well, but he seemed very trustworthy, and he always seemed approachable.

Keith led us to a small "side room" of the huge tent. There, he asked us what we understood from the lesson. We poured out the message that was so gently placed into our hearts that night.

"Are you really ready to have a personal relationship with Jesus and receive Him as your Lord and Savior tonight?" Keith asked us.

Derek and I looked at each other with resolve. "Yes," we affirmed.

"That's excellent. Then what we're going to do now is say a prayer for both of you at the same time, asking Jesus to come into your hearts and forgive you of all your sins. Are you ready?" Derek and I nodded in unison. "Great. Let's bow our heads together."

I closed my eyes and bowed my head the same way we always did in Sunday school. That time, however, I believed that particular prayer was different, and it would lead to a "personal relationship with Jesus Christ." The speaker that night made forgiveness sound so desirable, and I was ready to have my sins forgiven.

"Father in heaven," Keith began. "It's been a wonderful night. We thank you for the message that Derek and Lance have heard and responded to tonight. We know that we're sinners, and we need you to forgive us. Thank you for sending Jesus to die on the cross for our sins. Father, right now I just ask that you forgive Derek and Lance of all their sins, and that you will send Jesus to live in their hearts forever. We say this prayer in the name of your Son, Jesus Christ. Amen."

"Amen," we repeated, Derek doing so with tears in his eyes.

"Congratulations, brothers! I want to be the first to hug you guys as born-again believers." Keith wrapped us in a bear hug.

The ride home that night was consumed by our recounting of our salvation story. Derek's mom was enthralled. "I can't wait for you to tell your mom, Lance!"

Mom? I hadn't thought of her yet. What would she think? She knew that I had been going to church with Derek, but we never really seriously talked about it. The truth was, we rarely seriously talked about anything. It wasn't that we had a bad relationship. She just didn't dig for details, and I never provided any. Lying in Derek's room that night, trying to go to sleep, the one question that was on my mind was, *How come she never told me about salvation?* I didn't ask it in anger or sadness, but in curiosity.

That Sunday morning, Derek and I found out that we weren't the only ones who "got saved" on the previous Friday. Keith introduced Derek and me, as well as several others, to the class as "born-again" souls. That morning's lesson was my favorite lesson from Keith yet. He taught us that we would always be saved, now that we had Jesus living in our hearts. There was no way we could lose our salvation. That sounded great to me!

My mom and Mrs. Laura had become good talking buddies over the three years of my friendship with Derek.

They saw each other at least once a week, which was when either my mom would pick me up, or when Mrs. Laura would drop me off on Sunday evenings.

"Did you have fun?" my mom asked her standard question as Derek, Mrs. Laura, and I climbed the steps of our back porch from the driveway.

"Yep!" I answered, with extra enthusiasm.

"He and Derek got saved on Friday," Mrs. Laura responded with matched enthusiasm.

As my mother turned to look at me with questioning eyes, I was already leading Derek through the door, so we could raid the kitchen for whatever my mom had baked that weekend. After grabbing some cookies, we headed to my bedroom. We had already learned that, even though Mrs. Laura would leave the van running, her conversations with my mom on our back porch could last a half hour or longer.

After a span, "Come on, son!" came Mrs. Laura's voice through the hallway as she poked her head into the back door of the house.

"Congratulations," my mom offered, after Derek and Mrs. Laura had gone.

"Congratulations for what, Mamma?" my step-dad asked.

"He and Derek got saved at a church event this weekend."

"Oh. Good job, Bubba," he said.

And that was that. I still didn't know what my mom really thought, and I guess I would never find out. Either way, I supposed that was better than being interrogated.

The following months were generally positive. Derek and I continued in our Sunday school, he being the more active.

One day, he told me that he was going to get baptized on the coming Sunday.

"Cool. I was baptized as a baby," I replied. "What are you getting baptized for?"

"It makes me a real member of the Baptist Church," Derek replied.

"Well, I'll be there, of course!" I said, not really knowing if that was the best way to respond. I was happy for him. I just didn't know much about baptism.

The excitement was almost palpable in that maroon van that Sunday. The more Mrs. Laura affirmed her pride, and the more that Derek expressed his anxiety, the more excited I became. Derek and I eventually began treating his upcoming baptism as a rite of passage to manhood.

When the pastor announced Derek's decision, the whole church joined in our excitement. Then some assistants pulled on some cords, and a big baptistery was revealed behind the curtains behind the pulpit. I didn't know how Derek was going to get dunked under water inside the church until then.

Derek and the pastor disappeared behind a side door, and I waited with the rest of the church next to Derek's family for them to show up in the water. When they appeared, and after both Derek and the pastor said some really powerful words, the pastor let Derek fall backwards into the water. Derek went completely under without even plugging his nose! *Man, I would have had to plug my nose and look like a wimp in front of all these people!* I thought immaturely.

"That's much different from the way my dad's church baptizes," I told Derek, taking a bite of pizza a couple of hours later. We had gone to a pizza place to celebrate

Derek's baptism. Anytime that it was Derek's turn to choose what we ate, he always chose pizza. On this occasion, his whole family was there.

"How do they baptize?" Derek asked, wrinkling his nose.

"Baptism is just for babies, and the pastor puts his finger in a bowl of water and lets the water drip off his fingers onto the baby's forehead."

"That's weird."

I didn't know what to say, so I just stuffed some more pizza into my mouth. Was that weird? That was the way my sister and I were baptized. That was the way my parents were baptized. I was pretty sure that was the way my grandparents were baptized, too. I still didn't know much about baptism.

Soon after Derek's baptism, his parents gave me a very special gift. They had already proven their interest in my spiritual welfare by taking me to church almost every Sunday for several months. They really showed their care with their gift. "Merry Christmas. This is for you," Mrs. Laura said, handing me a leather pouch. "Open it up." I unzipped the bag and found a maroon Bible.

"Isn't that sharp? Now you'll have something to take to church with you on Sundays," Mr. Michael said in his "Deep South" accent.

That Bible really was a special gift. I still had the one from the Gideons from a little over a year prior, but this was the whole Bible, both the New Testament and the Old Testament. The new Bible was also much bigger. Below the date (December 1997), the dedication page said, "Love & Prayers—Trust Jesus and he will never let you down." Mrs. Laura and Mr. Michael really loved me.

The next few months were quite eventful with the local Baptist Church.

"Hey, we're having a lock-in next Friday!"

"What's a lock-in?" I asked Derek.

"It's where the whole youth group stays up all night together at the church, and you're not allowed to leave until the sun comes up the next day."

That sounded like fun! I went to church with Derek most Sundays, but he also went to church on Wednesday nights without me, so he always knew more about the events than I did.

The night of the lock-in was the very first time I had stayed up 24 hours straight. The boys mainly stayed up playing basketball in the church gym and *GoldenEye 007* for the Nintendo 64 in the youth room. It was a lot of fun.

Not long after the lock-in, I also attended my first revival. I didn't retain much about the content of the messages, but I definitely felt... revived!

Follow the Leader

1998; West Tennessee

"You've got to listen to what I found!" Derek exclaimed on the bus ride to his house. Derek was one of those lucky kids who, in my mind, was rich. He didn't live in a huge house, but his parents had good-paying jobs, and they handled their money well. Derek always had the new toys and gadgets. His family had recently gotten a new computer with Windows 98 and dial-up Internet.

When we got to his house, he booted up the computer and opened Real Player. He had downloaded some new music over the past week. He pushed *play*.

Derek was introducing me to a new music genre I had never heard. Little did I know that the music I was hearing would completely captivate the next several years of my life. The song playing on the computer was "Bradley" by a band named Coal Chamber. I loved how "dark" it sounded. The deep guitars sounded like they were growling and groaning, not to mention the raw vocals. It was such a change from the pop music I had listened to on my portable CD player that morning on the school bus. Plus, it was also the first music I had heard with really bad "cuss" words. That was appealing to a thirteen year old, who was in a hurry to grow up.

Derek clicked *stop* to prepare the next song. He was saving the best for last. When the chorus for "Freak on a Leash" by KoЯn broke out, I was hooked for good. At that moment, KoЯn became my favorite band, and they remained so for several years.

It wasn't long after that day in Derek's living room before I owned a t-shirt with KoЯn's *Follow the Leader* album artwork on it, which my girlfriend at the time had given to me. For the next five years or so, every shirt that I bought was black and promoted a band in the nü-metal scene. With that fashion style came chrome spikes, extremely baggy jeans, and on occasion, black fingernail polish.

Falling in love with heavy rock music also motivated me to learn how to play guitar. I had been a musician for a while, playing first trumpet in the school band, but there was no place for a trumpet in an aspiring metal rockstar's life. My mother bought my first guitar for me from a mail-order catalog for $69.

In November 1999, an album I greatly anticipated was released. At least a month in advance, I had asked my mother to purchase it for me on her way home from work on its release date. I was very specific that I wanted her to buy it from Target, though I didn't tell her why. Walmart only sold the "clean" versions of CDs, and I knew Target would sell the "unedited" version of the CD. On that day, she came home, handing me a Target bag with the album inside. I opened up the bag and retrieved the CD case with itching fingers. There was a note taped onto it.

"Son, I know that you're better than this."

She was referring to the disturbing album artwork, and especially the "Explicit Content" warning on the front. Any parent who had to watch her child completely transform the way I did as quickly as I did would have responded the way my mother did. She was concerned that her son was going off the "deep end."

Though I knew what came along with the "goth" image that I was portraying, the truth was, I had not rejected my belief in God whatsoever. In fact, as far as I saw it, it was stronger than it had ever been. Yet my mother knew better than I did that I was at a very impressionable age, and I was inviting a lot of temptation into my life.

I appreciated that my mother allowed me to make my own decisions regarding who I was and how people saw me. Unfortunately, since there really seemed to be no boundaries at all, I went to great and unnecessary lengths to express myself. They all began innocently enough, but they were transforming quickly. I had already proven to my family, my friends, God, and Satan that I was not afraid to try new things and to kick against what the world considered "normal."

Dark Experiments

Spring 2000; Henderson, Tennessee

My friend, Jared, was the first to introduce me to anything spiritual beyond Christianity. Of course, I had pondered the thoughts of Eastern religions and atheism, but my ignorance was enough grounds for me to reject those ideas. One day, in eighth grade math class, Jared handed me a book.

"Look at this"

"What is it?" I asked.

"It's a conjuration spell book."

"What's *Nec*-whatever?" I tried and failed to pronounce the word on the front of the book.

"It's a magic art that calls on dead people to work for you. There's a different conjuration for different things. Depending on what you want in life, you call on different souls."

"Do you really believe that stuff?" I questioned him.

"Yeah, it really works. Try it out."

I, being quite curious, took the book home to do as he suggested.

The first part of the book spoke of names and "words of power," outlining certain rituals that every conjuration required, regardless of whose spirit you were invoking. The rituals required symbols, candles, and a certain time of day. The book claimed that if you did everything right, the spirit would work in your favor, answering your specific prayer. This stuff was very intimidating and tempting at the same time.

What if it is true? I thought, sitting in my room with the door closed. I had recently been in an argument with a close friend. The book before me claimed to be able to solve it all, provided I get the spell just right. *I'm sure doing this wouldn't make God very happy. But if I am saved, isn't God with me? After all, I can't lose my salvation. Plus, if these spirits are evil, I can defeat them with God's power. Then God would be proud of me... Right?* I spent the rest of the night re-reading certain sections of the book so that I understood what I would be getting myself into. The entire time, however, my conscience worked against me, since I knew deep down that God did not want me tampering with the spiritual world in this way.

"Can I keep it for a few more days?" I asked Jared in math class the next day.

"Yeah, no problem. I've already read and memorized what I need to know."

I knew what he was talking about. He was talking about the names and the words of power. While performing the spell, the conjurer had to say the spell and names perfectly from memory. If he slipped up, he would be in a very dangerous position, being at the mercy of the powerful spirit.

"So, who have you called on?" I asked, trying to act as cool as he seemed.

"Can't tell you. Did you read that part?" Jared responded, reminding me that the book warned that the details of the ritual were just for the conjurer and no one else.

"Yeah, I was just curious. That's all."

"Take your time with the book. Just give it back when you're finished."

"Cool. Thanks."

By the end of the next day, I had accumulated the supplies prescribed by the book. I had also spoken to a few people, including my sister, about my discoveries in the book. All, without exception, warned me of how dangerous the spiritual realm is, and that it is not to be underestimated. In my defense, I told one person that I was so "confident in God" that I was ready to call upon Satan himself to face me. How immature I was!

My friends did not advise in vain. I delayed my incantation a few days, contemplating the warnings given. *Why would I do this, anyway?* Curiosity. To fit in with some of the goth culture. To impress some of my friends, particularly Jared. *Is it worth it?* I didn't want to find out. At that point, I resolved to remove this "magic" from my life as quickly as possible. I destroyed the drawings and candle I had prepared. The next day, I found Jared in the school hallway.

"Here. Thanks for letting me borrow it."

"Did you try it out?"

"Nah. Not for me," I tried to say nonchalantly. I was glad to be rid of the book.

Conformed

2000-2003; West Tennessee

My family was about to find out soon what was worse: a goth, a punk, or a pirate.

During my freshman year of high school, my friend, Zeike, and I started getting into the punk scene. He and I were listening to more and more bands that promoted drugs, anarchy, sex, vulgarity, and offense for the sake of offense. We still loved metal, but punk was growing on us quickly.

How much did the punk scene influence us? A lot, though I was convinced otherwise. I thought I was who I was only because of my own influence. I despised those who judged me. The punk scene influenced me deeply. The metal scene had influenced my wardrobe and my career choice (rock star), but the punk scene grabbed ahold of my inner being. It influenced me to experiment with drugs, theft, violence, and surface atheism (deep down, I never could deny the Creator; Romans 1:18-23). Thankfully, most of it was "experimental," and it did not become anything permanent. For a span, however, I was a brawler, a pseudo anarchist, a music and movie bootlegger, and the subject of many high school rumors.

I obtained my driver's license on September 26, 2001, ten days after my sixteenth birthday. My step-father had purchased a 1988 sport utility vehicle for me. I absolutely loved that thing. My mother, in her wisdom, gave me both freedom and responsibility when I started driving. Within reason, I could go wherever I wanted whenever I wanted. However, it was my responsibility to pay for my own gas and maintain my own car insurance. Of course, that required an income beyond the five to twenty dollars my mom had been giving me each week for spending money.

A few weeks after I obtained my driver's license, after school on a Monday afternoon, I walked into a local fast food restaurant and asked for an application. I was wearing a shirt promoting a notoriously vulgar musician. Since I had nowhere else to be, I ordered some food and filled out the application as I enjoyed my afternoon snack in one of the dining booths.

Luke was the manager on duty that day. Apparently, the restaurant needed help desperately. As I handed in my completed application, he invited me behind the "Employees Only" door, and he started to show me around. *Does he do this with every applicant?* I wondered after a few minutes.

"This is the breading machine, where you'll bread the chicken before cooking it," Luke explained. "And this is Hannah, who will be training you."

Just like that? I have a job? He hardly even looked at the application. What about an interview? "Oh, Hi, Hannah. It's nice to meet you," I said. I would have offered my hand, but she was busy cleaning out something very greasy.

"Nice to meet you. Love your shirt. He's my fave." We were going to get along just fine.

"Can you come in on Wednesday afternoon for orientation?" Luke asked me. "You'll get your uniform then."

"Yes, sir. No problem. I'll come right after school."

And that was it. I had a job with barely any effort. *This "real world" stuff is pretty easy*, I thought to myself. Starting then, my life began to change very rapidly. I had my license. I had freedom. I had my own money. What a combination for a sixteen-year-old!

Lighthouse Sessions

March 2003; West Tennessee

Most weekend evenings that I had off work, anyone could have found me with my friends in Jackson, Tennessee, enjoying some local bands at a hole in the wall place that most people referred to as the "Legion." As much as I enjoyed going there week after week, singing along to the music and moshing with my friends, my dream was to be on that stage. I had gotten pretty good at guitar, and I was looking for any opportunity to express myself with the music flowing through my veins.

"Did you know that Katie is playing at the Legion on Friday?" my friend, Andrea, asked me.

I had known Katie since the second grade, my first year in Tennessee. Andrea was our religiously agnostic mutual friend. Though she was agnostic, she was very open-minded. She and I had spent countless evenings on the phone discussing some very deep subjects.

"What?! No, I had no idea! Who is she playing with?"

"She's playing with this new punk band called Police King."

"I've never heard of them. I'm off work on Friday, so you

know I'll be there, anyway. How in the world did she join a band without telling me?"

That Friday evening, I arrived at the Legion before the first band went on, just like I always did. Everyone there knew me by name, which sometimes got me in for free. I glanced at the bill for the evening. There they were: "Police King—8:30." I started to look for Katie. Finding her, I asked, "So, you're playing tonight?"

"Yeah, we go on after the first band."

"Who's in your band? Do I know any of them?" I asked.

"Nah," Katie began. "They're some friends of a friend. I met them in Jackson last week. I'm not really 'in the band.' They've been around for a while, but tonight is their first time in Jackson. They have a new song that has a trumpet part in it. When they found out that I play trumpet, they asked if I would play that one song with them."

"So, you're like a ska band?" I asked.

"It's more like punk with a trumpet," Katie replied with a giggle.

"Cool. I look forward to hearing it!"

"Actually, I've told them about you," Katie said. "This band isn't permanent. Their singer-slash-guitarist is moving away next month. The remaining members want to start a new, permanent ska band. Their current drummer's going to sing, and they have another drummer lined up. They say he's really good. They want me to play trumpet, and their bassist is going to move to guitar—"

"Everyone's switching around like that?"

"Yeah. They're all talented and can play multiple instruments. I know you can, too, and that's where you come in. They're looking for a bassist."

"You told them I would play bass for them?" I asked, mouth agape.

"Yeah. I hope that's okay. I know how much you want to be in a band."

"That's perfect! You know I'm a guitarist, but I'm willing to play bass if it means I get to play music! Thanks! Introduce me later." Even before I heard them play, I was ready to sign my name to any dotted line if it meant I could play music.

Police King was even better than I expected. They were "fresh and flush," a phrase meaning that they were putting out new music, and they played it seamlessly—no start-overs, mess ups, bad notes, or angry looks at bandmates, all of which were common with these local bands. The song Katie played with them was the best out of all of them. She only played during the chorus, which was a nice touch.

After their lineup and while they were packing up their gear, I approached them.

"This is Bob, Mick, and Aaron," Katie said, introducing me to the band. "This is the guy I told you guys about," Katie said to the band.

Bob extended his hand. "So, you're our new potential bassist?"

"I hope so!" I said. "Man, your set was great tonight!"

"Thanks," Bob replied. "Aaron's moving away, so we need a new bandmate."

"I'd love to fill the gap."

"We'll see. We need to see how you play and how you can

work with us before we decide on anything."

"No problem. Where's the audition? I'll show you what I've got. I can play along to NOFX, the Sex Pistols, Dead Kennedys, and Blink-182." I saw a bit of recognition on Bob's face when I started to mention these punk bands, along with a bit of discomfort.

"There's one thing you need to know right away, Lance." Bob narrowed his eyebrows. "We're forming a Christian band."

I looked at Katie, whom I had never known to be religious. She was nodding. "No problem, Bob. I'm a Christian, too." I said enthusiastically, though the way I spoke and the way I was dressed likely gave him every reason to believe I was lying.

"Good," Bob said with a smile. "Can you meet us at the Beacon Apostolic Church on Tuesday at 8:00 pm? That's where we practice."

I thought about my work schedule before answering. "No problem, but where is it?"

Bob scrambled for a scrap piece of paper, found one, and wrote on it. "Here's the address. We need to pack up and head out now, so we'll see you then, okay?"

"Great. Thanks, guys!" I said, motioning to all the bandmates. "You were great tonight."

"See ya!" They said in unison.

Finding the address with no problem, I approached Beacon Apostolic Church at 7:45 pm. I had left with plenty of extra time, just in case I got lost. *Why are there so many cars here?* I thought as I pulled into the parking lot.

When I got out of the car, I could hear a lot of noise coming from inside the church. *Is that the band practicing? Are they putting on another show?* I slowly approached the building, and entered the main door. Walking down the hallway, I could comprehend the noise a bit better. It was a church service! *Is this their plan for tonight?* I thought with suspicion. I peeked inside the auditorium door, which was propped open. There were several people on stage, including a band. I didn't recognize most of the musicians, except that Bob was drumming. There were two people with microphones—a man and a woman—singing the same line over and over as the standing audience either joined them or shouted, "Amen!" and "Praise the Lord!" *This is weird*, I thought. I had never seen anything like it. *This must be the Pentecostal type church services I have heard about.*

It took me a few moments to notice Mick and Aaron at the back of the auditorium, standing near the door. A second after I noticed them, they noticed me.

"Hey, man! Come on over!" Mick shouted above the cacophony. I reluctantly joined them, trying not to seem as uncomfortable as I really was.

"Church started at 6:00," Aaron said. "We thought we'd be through by now, but we just kept going. This happens a lot. It should be over soon. The last songs are always the loudest. We'll start playing some music with you in no time. For now, just enjoy yourself and praise the Lord!"

There were people simply clapping to the rhythm, while others were raising and waving their hands, spinning in circles with their eyes closed. I feared for their safety. I could just imagine one of them stumbling over a pew or two of them heavily colliding.

As the band continued the same, hypnotic song, the man

who was obviously the pastor grabbed the microphone. The band kept the rhythm but quietened down a bit, providing dramatic background music for the pastor's speech.

"Isn't it wonderful, brothers and sisters—"

"Praise the Lord!" someone yelled from the crowd. "Thank you, Jesus!"

"—to come to God's house tonight?" the pastor continued. "The Holy Spirit has come upon us tonight!" The noise of everyone's speaking at once filled the place. I had never seen or heard anything like it.

The church service ended about thirty minutes after I arrived. "Hey, bro! Glad you found the place alright," Bob said, finding me and jumping off the stage. "Sorry. I thought we'd be done within two hours. We sometimes get carried away," he said with a shrug.

"Yeah, that's what Aaron said. No problem, though. Do you do this every night?"

"At least every Tuesday. We'll get started playing some tunes once everyone clears out."

We sat on a pew as we waited for the auditorium to clear out. We talked about music and our influences. Though I considered myself somewhat of a "music snob," my new friends listed a lot of bands I had never heard of before that night.

When we finally got to the instruments, I let the other guys warm up with some of their music. I listened for the melodies and bass lines. Before I picked up a bass guitar, I asked to play the six string. Doing all I could to impress them, I played some complicated punk riffs. Finally, picking up the bass guitar, I showed them what I had.

"Here, see if you can follow along," Mick suggested. He started playing something that sounded like reggae, punk, and jazz blended together. After about thirty seconds of observation, I tried keeping up.

"Nice, bro!" Aaron yelled over the loud amps. I looked over at Bob, and he was smiling, too.

Following the same procedure for the next thirty minutes, I proved that I could keep up with what these guys were pumping out.

"I think you're going to be just fine, man. How long have you been playing?" Mick asked me.

"Thanks. About five years. You guys are great, and I'd love to play some serious music with you all."

"Tell ya what," Bob started, "can you come back tomorrow night? We don't have church service, so we'll have some more time. I've already got Katie coming with Kemp, the new drummer."

Pausing to check my memorized work schedule the way I always did before any commitment, I finally responded, "Sure! What time?"

"Seven."

Between the two evenings, I was beaming. Finally, I had found worthy musicians, who were serious about making music. *Could this be it? Could I finally live my dream?* My "dream" was not based on fame. Sure, fame as a musician would have been great, but simply playing on the local stages with my friends, having people love my music the way I loved the local scene would have been enough for me.

The next evening came, and I was as excited as ever. When I walked into the auditorium, I found that Katie was already there with Andrea. It was strange seeing Andrea in a church, but I knew she didn't mind, and she would go wherever Katie went. I also saw the one who must have been Kemp. I didn't see Aaron anywhere. The other two boys were on the stage, Mick lazily lying down and Bob reading something from the Bible out loud. That was strange to me. I had never seen people my age actually read the Bible, much less read it to each other.

When I approached, Kemp stuck out his hand and said quietly, "Sup, bro. I'm Kemp."

"Lance."

"Ready to play music?" he asked, still courteously quiet for the Bible reading's sake.

"Yeah. As soon as everyone's ready."

After the Bible reading, Bob got up. "Alright! Let's start!"

Mick came up to me, and we slapped hands. "We try to read together most nights before we practice, especially when we are about to write some new tunes. It gets us in the right mindset."

"That's neat," I said, not knowing what else to say.

Everyone picked up his and her respective instruments. I was on bass guitar. Kemp was behind the drum set. Mick played guitar. Katie played the trumpet I had played next to for years in the school band. And Bob, claiming to do so for the first time ever, picked up the microphone.

There was an awkward "settling in" time in the beginning. I was new to them, and a few of us were playing instruments of second choice. We had different ways of warming up, and when it was time to start playing together, no one knew where to begin.

After about twenty minutes of "settling in," Mick got our attention. "Hey guys, check this out," he said, getting serious. "I've been working on this, and I showed it to Bob the other night. He's already working on a vocal piece. Facing Kemp, Katie, and me, Mick started hammering out an upbeat pop-punk piece. After he had shown us the main verse and chorus, he asked what we thought of it. I thought it was great, and I couldn't wait to see what I could come up with. Kemp replied by playing the beat he had come up with.

"What will I do?" Katie asked when Kemp was finished.

"I pictured you doing some melody during the chorus. It's in *E*. Do you think you can do it?" Mick replied.

"Yeah. Give me a while."

Mick and I spent the next twenty minutes working out what I could do to compliment the music, instead of just following the lead chords. Mick had excellent input. We came up with the most complicated bass line I had ever played at that point. I was excited!

Soon enough, Bob came in to show us what he had written for the lyrics and vocal melody. Katie had actually adapted the melody from a video game to insert into the chorus. By the end of the night, we had, for the most part, completed our first song together. Bob named it "Martyrs of Sinners." I was, at that point, officially part of a ska band.

The Recluse

March 2003; Henderson, Tennessee

A couple of weeks later, Katie asked me to meet her at Andrea's house. When the three of us were there, Katie said, "I got a call from Bob this morning. We can't use the church for practice anymore."

"What?"

"Yeah. Apparently we were playing music too late the other night, and the neighbors complained to Pastor John," she replied somberly.

"What are we going to do?" I asked.

"I don't know, but we're going to have to find a new place to practice."

"We've got to find something," I said desperately.

We sat there thinking for a while. After a long silence, Katie said, "Let's get out of here."

Katie, Andrea, and I then went to an ice cream shop and racked our brains for ideas on new practice pads. Andrea wasn't part of the band, but she was always around us. She didn't even like our type of music, but she was our biggest fan.

After a while, I was starting to think that all hope was lost. Finally, Katie said, "I've got a shed!" She said it chuckling, meaning it as a joke.

"Do you really? Does it have electricity?" I asked.

"Yeah, I think so. But that place is a dump. I don't think we can do anything with it."

"Where there's a will, there's a way," I said, trying to sound heroic. "Let's go check it out. Do you mind?"

"What else do we have to do? Let's go!" Katie said.

We finished our ice cream, and we were on our way. When we arrived, Andrea and I realized that Katie wasn't exaggerating with the word *dump*. We forced the door open and had our first look into her shed. There was a lightbulb hanging from the ceiling. Hoping against hope, I climbed over the piles of garage sale stuff, bags of clothes, boxes of books, and piles of unorganized stuff. I reached for the pull string, and to our amazement, the bulb came on.

I looked around, and I also found three electrical outlets. "This place is perfect! Do you think your mom will care?"

"Nah. She's really easy-going."

"Great! Let's get to work!"

By the end of that evening, we had cleared out the junk, swept up the dust, and moved in some music equipment. The place was infested with bugs. Joking, Andrea suggested that the shed should be called *the Recluse* because of all the brown recluse spiders we had to sweep out of the place. The name stuck, and from then on, the little shed in Katie's back yard was *the Recluse*.

A couple of days later, we had moved a drum set, PA

system, and some guitar amps into the Recluse. After Mick read something from the Bible, we had our first band practice in the Recluse. Katie made the rule that, since her neighbors were so close in proximity, we would have to stop playing at 9:00 pm.

Though it was "amps off" time at 9:00, we hung out until after midnight in the Recluse that first night. We spent the time talking about every subject under the sun. It was also that night that I decided that if we were going to spend so much time reading the Bible together, I should put more effort into paying attention, trying to understand, and even give my input every now and then when the passage was discussed.

After fatigue had set into many of us and things were getting quiet, Bob blurted, "No Hit Wonder."

"Huh?" Kemp and I asked.

"That's the band name I've come up with. What do you think?"

We were trying to be a ska band that people didn't take too seriously, yet we wanted to make music that was enjoyable and meaningful, not comedic. "I think it fits," I said.

"I'm just the drummer," Kemp said, smiling and shrugging.

"He's already asked me, and I told him I like it," Mick said.

Katie started giggling. We all looked at her and waited for her to explain herself. Her giggling crescendoed into laughter for a few seconds until she could contain herself. It was clearly after midnight. "It's perfect!" she blurted, right before another fit consumed her. Katie was the type of person who was able to find meaning in the smallest things and humor in the blandest things, especially while sleep-deprived.

From then on, we were known as No Hit Wonder, the ska band with only one brass instrument. That night started a very regular ritual of "burning the midnight oil" in the Recluse.

Toe Socks and a Cowboy Hat

March - April 2003; Henderson, Tennessee

"This is Devin," Luke said as I came into work one day. "Today is his first day. Why don't you show him around?"

Devin was a tall, blonde guy with a distinct mole on his left cheek. He looked to be a few years older than I was. Because of my sister and brother-in-law, I knew almost everyone who had graduated from Chester County within the past six years. Why hadn't I seen him around before? *He must be new to town.*

"Nice to meet you, Devin. We're on chicken duty tonight. Come on back."

Devin caught on quickly. He seemed like a cool guy, too. There was something different about him, though. I couldn't figure it out. He didn't talk like he was from Henderson. He also didn't seem to fit the bill of someone who would work at a fast food restaurant. *What is it that is so different about him? I'll figure it out eventually.*

"So, what year were you?" I asked Devin.

"High school?"

I nodded.

"2000 in Texas. I should graduate Freed in 2005."

That was one of the things that was different about him. "Freed" was short for "Freed-Hardeman University," the center of Henderson, Tennessee. During the school year, Henderson was busy. During the summer, it seemed dead. Freed was a Christian-based school and the butt of many jokes by the locals, or "townies," as the "Freedies" referred to us.

"Ah, so you're a college student," I said. "I'll graduate high school next year. Then I plan to go to University of Tennessee in Martin."

"What do you plan to major in?" Devin asked.

"Graphic Design. What are you majoring in?"

"Computer Science. I'm getting married in August. That's why I applied for the job here. I need a bit of cash before the wedding."

"Wow. That's cool. What's her name?"

"Wendy," he said, pulling out his wallet to show me a picture of his brunette fiancée.

"So, what can you do with a Computer Science degree?" I asked while removing the chicken bucket from the walk-in freezer.

"Mainly, I'll be able to design computer programs and video games."

"Aw, that sounds sweet. A few years ago, I wanted a career in video game testing. It didn't take me long to realize how unrealistic that dream was, but I still think it would be fun."

From then, Devin and I talked about our tastes in video games, which led us to discuss movies and Internet comics. We were going to get along great.

Devin was my first friend from Freed-Hardeman University. From what I had been told, Freedies were stuck up and judgmental. Not this guy. However, I did learn a few things that were strange about him, like he was the only guy I ever knew to be proud of wearing toe socks on a regular basis, and he wore a cowboy hat to work until he had to switch it out for his company hat. He also read fantasy novels instead of gossiping and/or smoking cigarettes on his dinner breaks.

It didn't take long for Devin and me to learn each other's strengths and weaknesses at work, which turned us into a great team. Most people working at a fast food joint don't take their job very seriously. Although he didn't plan to turn it into a career, Devin was committed to working hard at what he did. He inspired me to do the same. We challenged each other, sometimes competing who could do the best job the fastest. The managers of the restaurant took notice, and they started scheduling us together on a regular basis, which was great for our developing friendship.

Love and Justice

Thursday, July 10, 2003; Henderson, Tennessee

At band practice one day, during one of our fifteen minute breaks, I asked Bob, "So, what's it mean?" He and I were the only ones in the Recluse. The rest had walked the five minutes down the road to the local grocery store to buy some sodas for the crew. The vending machines still sold their twelve ounce cans for 50 cents each. "You know, 'Martyrs of Sinners.' I really like the song, but I can't hear what you're saying much over the drums and amps."

"Well, you know what a martyr is, right?"

Bob could tell I didn't by the look on my face.

"It's someone who dies for what he believes in. The idea of the song is that the world is so caught up in sin, that sin is all the world knows. We're taught by the world to be tolerant of sin and to not judge and all that. The world thinks that sin is so important that they would rather die defending their sinful lives than to look at their lives the way God does and change accordingly."

"Well, isn't that why Jesus died on the cross?" I asked. "He died for their sins."

"The thing is, Jesus died for everyone's sins," Bob

continued, "yours and mine included. But the question is *why* did he have to die? Have you ever thought of that? Most people who believe in Jesus go around saying that Jesus died for their sins, but they're only willing to talk about the love of God. Don't get me wrong, the Bible says that God is love and all, but the Bible also says that God is a just judge. Most people know John 3:16 real well, 'For God so loved the world, that he gave his only Son—'"

"Yeah, I know that verse," I said with recognition. "The first time I ever saw it was in a family member's house in Michigan. She had it hanging in a picture frame in her kitchen."

"But here's the deal, man. Can you tell me why God sent his Son to die? That doesn't sound very loving to me."

"Well, you're right," I said. "If I hadn't heard what you just said, I would have said because he loves us."

"That's right, since the Bible says so. But if you keep going on like that, it becomes circular reasoning. God loves you, so he sent his Son. Why? Because he loves you; therefore, he sent his Son. You see? So, what's the other part of it?"

"I guess it has something to do with justice, doesn't it?" I asked, thinking back to what Bob said about God being a loving, yet a just judge."

"You got it, bro! What did God tell Adam and Eve would happen if they disobeyed him?" Bob asked.

"Man, I don't remember. I was just a kid when I learned about that. All I know is they took the apple from the snake, and that was bad."

"No problem. The reason why it was sinful was because God told them not to do it, not because eating fruit is bad. Anyway, God told them that if they ate of that one tree, despite the fact that he had provided them the rest of the entire Garden to get food from, they would die. He was not only talking about physical death in the future, but he was talking about spiritual death right then and there, at the moment of the first sin."

"Wow. I do remember now. I feel like I would know better than to take food from a snake anyway." I responded with a chuckle.

"Give them the benefit of the doubt, man. Things were much different then. You're right, though. They never should have done it. Tell me; how would you describe the best judge in the state?"

"*Honest* would be number one," I answered. "He would make sure the baddies got locked away."

"So, a good judge punishes evil, right?"

"Yeah, sure." I said.

"By which standard? I mean, how does he know who deserves what? And how consistent should he be, since he is a good judge?"

"He uses the law to punish criminals, and if the crime is clear, then the judge should always be consistent with punishment."

"True that," Bob agreed. "Now, think about this. God said that Adam and Eve would face death when they sinned. We also know that God loves everyone. What if God would have said, 'Aw, it's no big deal. I love you so much that I won't punish you like I said I would'?"

"I guess that would have made him a liar and a bad judge at the same time. Is that what you're getting at?" I asked.

"Precisely! But, thankfully, that's not the end of it! We also know that God is all-powerful, right?"

I nodded.

"Ok, so what if he just left Adam and Eve to suffer both spiritual and physical death without offering any help? He's all-loving and all-powerful, yet he does nothing to help them."

"That wouldn't make any sense!" I said, understanding where Bob was going.

"That's right, and do you know we're in the same boat as Adam and Eve?" Bob asked.

"What do you mean?"

"I've sinned just like them. Haven't you?"

"Yeah," I admitted. "A lot!"

"And the Bible says that the punishment for sin is...?" Bob said, inflecting his voice at the end.

"Death!"

"Now, think about that in connection with John 3:16. God sent his Son because he loves us," Bob paused for effect. "But why did he have to send him in the first place?"

"Because of our sins," I said somberly. "It's true that Jesus never sinned, right?"

"Right, and that's how he was in the position to die for our sins. Let me ask you, Lance; since we have sinned, what is it that you and I deserve?"

"We deserve to die, I guess. But I don't feel like I'm as bad as a murderer or a rapist or anything."

"That's not the point, man. Did Adam and Eve kill or rape anyone before God had to keep his promise?"

"I've never thought of it that way," I said.

"So, now that you and I both know that we have both sinned and that we both deserve death, do you think God would let me take your punishment for you?"

"No, he wouldn't, since we both deserve the same thing, right?"

"Correct," Bob pointed out. "Just like Adam had to face punishment *with* Eve, and not *instead* of Eve. So, how does Jesus come into the picture?" Bob asked with raised eyebrows.

It hit me. I had never thought about it before, but it was as clear as clear could be. I felt like I understood God for the first time in my life. He loved me, and he made a big sacrifice to prove it. "He could die for our sins because he never sinned! He never deserved the punishment of death, yet he died so that we don't have to!" For my whole life, I had done what most people did. I stated the "circular statement of Christianity." Jesus died for our sins because he loved us, so he died for our sins because he loved us. I had never thought of God's justice like this before. There was a perfect balance.

The rest of the band showed up with their caffeine fixes. Mick handed Bob and me our drink orders.

"Ok, but we haven't finished yet." Bob said, cracking open his soda can.

"Finished what?" Katie asked.

"We were just having a discussion about the love and justice of God," Bob answered.

"Sounds deep," Katie said.

"What else is there?" I asked Bob.

"Again, what does John 3:16 say?" Bob asked me.

"I know that one!" Katie chimed. "For God so loved the world, that he gave his only begotten Son, that whosoever believeth in him should not perish, but have everlasting life," she quoted from the King James Version.

Bob looked at Katie and raised an eyebrow. "That was good!"

"Yeah, my grandmother taught it to me when I was young. I've remembered it ever since."

"Here's the big question," Bob said, looking back at me. "Does God force people to be saved, or does he give them a choice?"

"I guess we all have to choose, right?" I said, a bit unsure.

"Yep. God doesn't produce robots. That's not love, is it? If you were brainwashed to tell your mother you love her, would that be real love?"

"No."

"It's the same with God. He wants us to love him, but we can choose not to. Going back to John 3:16, on what grounds does God offer salvation? How do do people accept eternal life?"

"They've got to believe in Jesus."

"Good job," he said, standing up. "And it's a choice we all have to make."

Kemp was already behind his drum set, and Mick was strapping on his guitar. I picked up my bass guitar.

"You remember how we got on this subject?" Bob asked.

After a moment, I did. "I asked about the song."

"Yeah. I told you that the world loves being sinful, and

you said that's what Jesus died for. You were right, but now do you understand that the world is in a dangerous place, being where they are? God's not going to force these people into heaven. They've got to accept it on God's terms. That's why we do what we do. Now, come on, and let's play some music."

That night, I could hardly sleep. I was thinking about what Jesus had done for me. Being around Bob, Mick, and Kemp made me want to change for the better. They made Christian living look fun. They could let loose, laugh, play video games and music, and almost everything else without having to cuss, drink, break the law, offend, or "fit in" with the rest of the world. They were completely comfortable being who they were. I wasn't. For the first time in my life, I stepped back and really gazed into the life that I was living. I had spent the last several years fooling myself. I had told myself and the people around me that I didn't care what people thought of me. The reason why I said that was because I wanted them to think highly of me. How hypocritical. I tried to fit in by standing out. By offending. By hurting. By going against the grain. I thought I was unique, but everyone that I hung out with was doing the same thing. Everyone except for the guys of No Hit Wonder.

After Hours

Friday, July 11, 2003; Henderson, Tennessee

I had to work the next evening. A few minutes before break time, Katie came into the restaurant. It only took her five minutes to walk to the restaurant from where she lived.

"Hey, what's up?" I asked her.

"Just came for some grub. When's your break?"

"You're just in time. I get my dinner break in a few minutes."

"Great," she said. After ordering her food, she said, "I'll be over there."

I ordered my food and clocked out when our orders were finished. "What's up?" I asked, sliding into the opposite side of the booth as Katie.

"Nothing really, I just wanted to get the chance to talk to you while not around the guys. They're different, aren't they?" She asked.

"Yeah. I was thinking a lot about that last night."

"They remind me of my grandmother, someone who really takes God seriously," she said. "My mom raised me to believe in God and stuff, but my grandmother takes it real seriously, you know?"

"Yeah, I do. I feel extra righteous around those guys. It's strange saying that I'm in a Christian band now, but I'm happy about it. I feel like it could go somewhere, and we can change some lives."

"Yeah," Katie said. "I feel like this band is changing my life, though."

We talked about a few other things while we finished our dinners. "When do you get off?" she asked.

"I'm closing tonight."

"Come on down when you're finished. I think the guys are gonna be there."

The restaurant closed at 9:00 pm, and we had the "good" crew working that night, including Devin, so we were finished with lock up and clean up at 9:30. After clock out, I went to the Recluse. All of the band was there, plus Andrea. Even though it was too late to play music, I had grown to really enjoy hanging out with the band "after hours," and I was glad Katie suggested I come by.

We spent some time talking about music concepts. We let the conversation drift from subject to subject. Later that night, Mick said to me, "You know, you should come to church with us."

I knew that was going to come up some time. "Yeah, I suppose I should. I'm just not used to that type of service."

"What, the speaking in tongues and stuff?" Mick asked.

"Yeah," I said carefully with a grin, not wanting to offend him.

"I know what you mean, man. It's really weird the first

time you see it, but you should experience it yourself. Then you'll know what it's all about."

"Why do you guys do it, anyway? I don't mean to be mean, but it just sounds like gibberish to me." I spoke a bit bolder than before.

"I know what it sounds like to an outsider, but to us who have faith, it's the best thing in the world. We're talking to God when we speak in tongues. So, I guess you've never received the Holy Spirit?"

"I always thought I had the Holy Spirit. I mean, my youth pastor told me I did many years ago, but I've never spoken in tongues."

"Come to church with us on Tuesday night. See what happens."

I thought about my work schedule, hoping that I had to work on Tuesday. "We'll see," I said, not willing to admit that Tuesday was the only day off I had within the next week.

Disappointing Diet Restrictions

Sunday, July 13, 2003; Henderson, Tennessee

I was on dining duty on the following Sunday night. That meant that I was one of the workers in the front, taking customers' orders. Devin never worked Sundays, so it was one of the few evenings he and I weren't scheduled together since we joined food forces.

"My mom and grandmother are coming up here in just a little bit, so I'll want to go on break then," Tina, the other dining worker, said to me as things were slowing down after the dinner rush.

"Works for me," I said.

A few minutes later, Tina said, "Here they are. Will you take their order?"

"Sure, no problem. Hello, ladies," I said, turning to Tina's mother and grandmother. We've got the bacon cheeseburger on special tonight, would you like one of those?"

"We don't eat bacon," Tina said, clocking out at the other register.

"Oh, okay. Sorry about that. What could I get you?"

Thirty minutes later, Tina said goodbye to her family and clocked back in.

"If you don't mind my asking, why don't you eat bacon? Besides the milkshakes, it's the best thing on the menu," I said to Tina.

"The Bible forbids it," she said.

I literally jumped back in shock, stunned for a few seconds. I had never heard of that, but she said it like it was common knowledge. I had heard that certain Eastern religions had strict diets, but I never heard of Christians having diet rules, at least as far as meat went. "What? Really? Where?"

"Leviticus chapter eleven," she said with no apparent trouble remembering. "You should check it out."

"Believe me; I will." I loved bacon. I had no idea that the Bible told me not eat it, but if that's what the Bible said, there was a change coming in my diet. If my life was going to change, as I had recently resolved, I had to take this stuff seriously. I grabbed a napkin and tried to write the Scripture reference down. "What was that verse again?" I asked Tina.

"Leviticus chapter eleven. It's the third book of the Bible."

That's what I wrote down. "Third book. Chapter eleven." I had never heard of *Levit*-whatever before.

That night, I dug in my nightstand to find the maroon Bible with its leather case that Derek's family had given to me several years prior. Finding the eleventh chapter of the third book, I started reading. There it was. Verses seven and eight.

And the pig...is unclean to you. You shall not eat...

Why has no one ever taught this to me? It was so clear in my own Bible. Not only that, but using words like *cud* and *hoof* among the pig, the Bible also described several other animals that should not be eaten. *So, Christians are to have a strict diet, too. There are a lot of people not following this passage. I'm going to start following it right now,* I thought.

Unexpected Lesson

Monday, July 14, 2003; Henderson, Tennessee

The next day, Devin and I were back on the schedule together again. He was on chicken duty, and I was on grill. At his break time, he called back, ordering the bacon cheeseburger that was on special.

"You might not want to do that, man," I called back to him.

"Why not? You looking after my health?" He asked, rubbing his belly with a smile.

"Nah," I said chuckling. "The Bible says bacon's unclean, and we shouldn't eat it. You go to a Christian college. You should know that!" I was quite proud of myself. There I was teaching someone what the Bible said. I had certainly never done that before.

"What are you talking about, man? That's part of the old covenant of Moses," Devin responded.

That sounded like a trump card. "The old what?"

"The old covenant, you know, the Law of Moses."

"The Bible's the Bible, man. You're supposed to do what it says. It's that simple...right?"

"Yes," Devin began. "But you have to read each verse in context. That's the downfall of most people's interpretation today. Most people just want to read out one verse and start applying it to their life and everyone else's life. Have you ever walked through a crowd before and just heard a tiny bit of a conversation? Like, you hear just one sentence of what someone says, and it sounds really weird to you?"

"Yeah, that happens at school all the time," I admitted. "It's really funny, because I walk away, and try to see if I can fill in the gaps with the funniest scenarios."

"I know what you mean. But, you know, that's what people are doing with the Bible. God has an entire message to deliver, and if we look at just a few verses in the middle, ignoring the passages before it and after it, we could be putting ourselves in a lot of danger."

"Okay. I get what you're saying. So, you think that's what I did with the pig passage?"

"I'll tell you what," Devin said, looking out into the dining room. "It's pretty slow right now. I bet Luke would let you take your break with me. Could I show you a few things over dinner?"

"Yeah, that would be great!"

Devin always carried his backpack into work and kept it and his cowboy hat on the coat hooks right behind the "Employees Only" door. A few minutes later, Devin, his backpack, and I were sitting at the break bar for the employees near the back door. He pulled a Bible out of his bag.

"Do you always carry that with you?" I asked.

"Yeah. I'm taking a Bible class at Freed, so it's one of my textbooks, but I love having my Bible with me. It's helpful in times like this. You ready?"

"Yep."

He turned to the book of Leviticus. "I have a feeling you were talking about something you had read from this book. True?"

"Yeah. Tina actually told me about it yesterday. I had never even heard of that book before she told me about her family's diet. Here it is, open in front of me again."

"Like I said, though," Devin started, "you've got to read all things in their context. If you were to look at the first five books of the Bible, you would see most of the exciting stories we hear about in Sunday school, like Adam and Eve, Noah, the Tower of Babel, Abraham, Joseph, and Moses. Do you remember ever learning about them?"

"My friend and I were talking about Adam and Eve and God's justice and love just the other day. I vaguely remember the others, but yeah, I've heard of them, especially Noah with the ark."

"Ok, that's a great start. For learning what I hope to show you tonight, you really just need to know about Moses. God sent Moses to Egypt to free the entire nation of Israel from slavery. That's when Moses parted the Red Sea. Do you remember that?"

"Oh, yeah! I said with recognition. "I have a movie at home about that. I think the guy that does Darth Vader's voice does a voice in that movie, too. Man, I haven't even thought of that movie since I was a kid!"

Devin shook his head. "Darth Vader in the Bible. That's a funny picture. Well, anyway, after Moses and the Israelites went through the parted sea, God led them to a mountain, where God gave Moses a law to give to the Israelites. Look at this." He turned to Deuteronomy 5. "Can you read verses 1 through 3 for us?" Devin took a bite of his burger and turned the Bible for me to read. Out of courtesy, he ordered a burger without bacon on it.

"Sure."

> *And Moses summoned all Israel and said to them, "Hear, O Israel, the statutes and the rules that I speak in your hearing today, and you shall learn them and be careful to do them. The LORD our God made a covenant with us in Horeb. Not with our fathers did the LORD make this covenant, but with us, who are all of us here alive today."*

"What did Moses say God made?" Devin asked.

"A covenant, but what's a covenant?"

"It's an agreement between two parties. It's kind of like a contract. The word *covenant* is the same thing as a *testament,*" Devin answered. "And with whom did God make this covenant?"

"It says God made it with us," I answered, feeling somewhat accomplished.

"Context. One of the very best ways to determine context is to ask two questions. First, who is speaking here?"

"Moses is."

"Second, to whom is he speaking?"

"Us," I said.

"Be careful," Devin cautioned, pointing at me with a French fry. "Look again at verse one. What does it say?"

I read the verse out loud again, which changed my answer. "Moses was speaking to the nation of Israel!"

"Exactly," Devin said with a smile, looking accomplished himself. "Are you from Israel?" he asked me.

"Nope."

"Just because you see the word *us*, don't assume that it includes you. One of the biggest mistakes people make when trying to understand the Bible is that they always think the Bible is talking to them when they see the words *us* or *you*. Sometimes it is intended for us all, but sometimes it's not. We've got to always ask those questions: 'Who is speaking?' and 'To whom is he or she speaking?' On this occasion, Moses was announcing the new law that God was giving to the nation of Israel. Included in that law are the commandments found in the book of Leviticus."

"So, what do you mean? Those commandments aren't for us?" I asked, probably looking a bit confused. I had never thought about the Bible in this way. Although I knew the Bible told stories of history, I had still aways looked at the Bible as a simple and straight-forward list of dos and don'ts.

"That's a really good question, but I don't want to outright tell you the answer. I want the Bible to answer it for you." He turned his Bible to the book of Jeremiah. Finding chapter 31 and verse 31, he said, "Jeremiah lived about 600 years before Jesus was born on the earth, which was during the Law of Moses. Read verse 31."

> *"Behold, the days are coming," declares the LORD, "when I will make a new covenant with the house of Israel and the house of Judah."*

After I had read the verse, Devin asked, "What was it that God promised through Jeremiah, and what do you think he was talking about?"

"He said he would make a new covenant. Is that the New Testament?" I asked.

"Yep. Remember that *covenant* and *testament* mean the same thing. Let's look at what the New Testament says about all of this." Devin turned to Hebrews 8. "The Hebrews author wrote this after Jesus' death and resurrection. He says in verse six that Jesus brings a new and better covenant. He then spends verses eight through twelve quoting the passage we just looked at in Jeremiah. Now, read verse thirteen."

> *In speaking of a new covenant, he makes the first one obsolete. And what is becoming obsolete and growing old is ready to vanish away.*

"Whoa!" I exclaimed.

"What does this mean?" Devin asked me.

"It means that the old covenant, the Old Testament, has been made obsolete! It's outdated," I said with understanding.

"That's right," Devin affirmed. "In the Old Testament, if someone wanted the forgiveness of sins, that person had to offer animal sacrifices. What does the New Testament teach about the forgiveness of sins?"

"It's through the sacrifice of Jesus Christ," I answered.

"Precisely. There were some Christians in Galatia that were trying to mix both the old Law with the law of Christ. The apostle Paul wrote to them to warn them what they were doing. Look at this." Devin pointed to Galatians 5:3.

> *Look: I, Paul, say to you that if you accept circumcision, Christ will be of no advantage to you. I testify again to every man who accepts circumcision that he is obligated*

to keep the whole law.

"There were people in the church," Devin continued, "who were trying to be saved by following the works of the Law of Moses, like circumcision. What two things does Paul say concerning those who want to do that?"

"Christ would not be an advantage to them, and they would have to keep all of the Law. What does he mean?" I asked.

"I want to show you that the Bible works best when it answers your questions. I think this passage can help you understand." Devin pointed to Galatians 3:10-11 on the previous page.

> *For all who rely on works of the law are under a curse; for it is written, "Cursed be everyone who does not abide by all things written in the Book of the Law, and do them." Now it is evident that no one is justified before God by the law, for "The righteous shall live by faith."*

"So," I began, "if you accept one thing from the Law, you have to accept it all, right?"

"Right you are!" Devin said with a nod. "Which also means you're rejecting the law of Christ. Look back at chapter five, and re-read verse two."

> *Look: I, Paul, say to you that if you accept circumcision, Christ will be of no advantage to you.*

"Think about it this way," Devin said. "If you accept one thing from the old law, you have to accept it all, which includes animal sacrifices for sins, right?"

I nodded.

"How do you think it would make Jesus feel if we said, 'We don't need your sacrifice, because we have the blood of bulls and goats'?"

"I'm sure it would make him mad!" I said.

"Not only would it make him mad, but it would also break his heart. He showed his love by sacrificing himself. To say that would be to reject his love."

"Wow. I never thought of the Old and New Testaments this way," I said while Devin was turning to a new passage. It was Hebrews 10:3-4.

"This is what the Hebrews author wrote about animal sacrifices contrasted with the sacrifice of Christ."

> *But in these sacrifices there is a reminder of sin every year. For it is impossible for the blood of bulls and goats to take away sins.*

"It would not only upset Christ if we relied on animals, but it would also be eternally dangerous to our souls. Remember that passage in the book of Leviticus that gave diet restrictions to the nation of Israel? Look at what Jesus said in Mark 7:18-23."

> *And he said to them, "Then are you also without understanding? Do you not see that whatever goes into a person from outside cannot defile him, since it enters not his heart but his stomach, and is expelled?" (Thus he declared all foods clean.) And he said, "What comes out of a person is what defiles him. For from within, out of the heart of man, come evil thoughts, sexual immorality, theft, murder, adultery, coveting, wickedness, deceit, sensuality, envy, slander, pride, foolishness. All these evil things come from within, and they defile a person."*

"This is why the Hebrews author quoted Jeremiah saying that God's new covenant would be concerned more about the heart than the stone the Law was written on," Devin added.

"So, this must mean we can eat bacon, huh?" I asked.

"You tell me."

"If I understand it correctly, we can."

"First, I want to say that you are correct, and you always have an opportunity to understand God's word. Be careful not to pull Scriptures out of context. Don't let other people do that, either. Second, I want to say that the covenant that has been made obsolete was the Law of Moses, which can be found in the form of commandments in the Old Testament. That does not mean that everything in the Old Testament has been made obsolete. For example, it's still true that 'In the beginning, God created the heavens and the earth,' right?"

"Yeah, I understand."

"We can still learn a whole lot from the Old Testament. The book of Proverbs includes teachings that will be true for eternity. We can also see God's providence in the lives of so many Old Testament people."

"How did you learn so much?" I asked. "Are you sure you're going to school to be a computer nerd and not a pastor?"

"I'm sure I'm going to be a computer nerd. I learned this stuff about the Bible two different ways. First, I spend time reading it on my own. Second, I had a dear friend in my life a few years ago that was willing to do what I'm doing for you right now. I appreciate your attitude and willingness to accept Scripture as is."

I was impressed, to say the least. Devin was proving to be more than a good buddy. He had just done for me what no one else was willing (or perhaps, able) to do. He answered a need in my life with an open Bible. People had referenced the Bible and quoted Scripture to me before, but no one prior to that day had actually opened the Bible and said, "Look here for yourself."

Pushing Faith

Tuesday, July 15, 2003; West Tennessee

The phone rang the next day. "Are you planning on going to church tonight?" Katie asked after I picked up the phone and greeted her.

"I don't know. Probably not."

"Well, I want to go, and I need a ride. I was hoping you were going," Katie said.

"Well, when you put me on the spot like that..."

"Come on, it'll be fun! What would you be doing, anyway?" She had a point.

When I arrived at Katie's house, I was surprised to see Andrea there. She was planning to go to church, too. Fifteen minutes later, we arrived in the parking lot just in time to hear the band kick up. "At least I love live music," I told the girls, trying to find something to be excited about. I was actually a bit uneasy. The only other time I had seen this type of stuff was when I stumbled upon it a few weeks earlier, intending only to audition for a rock band.

Thirty minutes later, after some music, I was on the very back pew with Andrea and Katie, listening attentively to the testimonies that people in the congregation gave. They told powerful stories from the previous week that either made the listeners, including me, want to cry or get up and do something for the Lord.

"Amen!" "Hallelujah!" "Thank you, Jesus!" came the replies.

After the testimonies, Mick and Kemp joined us on the back pew. Bob was on stage with the band. Pastor John and his wife then began delivering a powerful message. I had never heard so much energy in a sermon before. In the middle of their message, Pastor John said, "God is telling me something right now. Somebody came in here tonight doubting. I want everyone to stand up right now."

While complying, Katie and I looked at each other, both of us wondering who God was "talking" about. I wondered if it was Andrea.

"Do you want God to prove Himself to you tonight?" the pastor continued while the band started playing softly. "He wants to prove Himself to you!"

Most of the people were standing with eyes closed and hands raised high. Some of the bodies were swaying back and forth. Some people were waving their hands. A man wearing a red shirt stepped out into the aisle.

"I want Him to prove Himself to me!" he cried out over the racket.

"Come on down, son," the pastor said, grabbing the cordless microphone and stepping off the stage. "Tonight, you're going to receive the Holy Spirit. Come on over here." He motioned to the man in the aisle and to the men on the front pews, who were obviously his helpers. The pastor and his helpers surrounded the man in what looked like a football huddle. Placing their hands on the man's head and shoulders, the team all started speaking in a muddled speech, and the band on stage heightened their volume and tempo.

Into the microphone, the pastor prayed, "Jesus, send your Spirit upon this one tonight. Let Him feel your presence." The pastor repeated the same prayer over and over for at least a minute. Finally, the man in the middle raised his hands and began to slowly fall to his knees. After another moment, he was slumped on the ground. It appeared like he was convulsing.

"This man has the Spirit!" the pastor proclaimed to the church.

The clamor rose to new heights. Soon enough, the man was back into his pew, happily praising God with his friends, sweat showing through his red shirt.

"You see?" Mick said, referring to what had just happened.

I slowly nodded with wide eyes in response.

"Who else has doubt tonight?" the pastor asked, gazing over the fifty or sixty of us in the auditorium. "Someone else has come in here doubting. I know it. God is telling me."

No one responded beyond the regular shouts of praise. The pastor went back to the lectern, and the band quieted down. After instructing us all to sit back down, he and his wife continued their collaborated sermon. I couldn't focus on the rest of the sermon. Instead, I replayed in my head what I had just seen. *That was real*, I told myself. My thoughts were broken as the pastor motioned for the band to pick it up again.

"Who is it that God is calling tonight?" the pastor asked, wireless microphone in hand again. For the second time, the whole church stood in unison, hands raised high.

Mick motioned for me to stand up, and I did, Katie following suit.

"Relax," Mick said. "Go with the flow. Stop shunning the Spirit."

I closed my eyes and allowed the music to control the sway of my body. The music was almost hypnotic. I thought of the man in the red shirt. I thought of my times reading the Bible with the guys and Katie in the Recluse. Back and forth my body swayed.

As the music and the swaying continued, I felt Mick's hand land on my right shoulder. I raised my hands. Another hand planted on my left shoulder, and I could feel someone standing in front of me. I assumed it was Kemp, but I didn't want to open my eyes. A minute later, I was in the middle of a football huddle.

"Block everything else out," the pastor said, speaking only to me. He continued, "Have faith that you will receive the Spirit tonight. Whenever you're ready, just let your mouth flow."

Speaking into the microphone, Pastor John started, "Jesus, send your Spirit upon this one tonight. Let Him feel your presence." The surround sound muddle began.

I muttered. I stammered. I did all I could to "have faith," just as the huddle commanded. I let my tongue "flow." Nothing beyond my control flowed from it. I felt dizzy. *Is that the Holy Spirit?* I felt weak in the legs. *Is that the Holy Spirit?* I gave way under the emotional and physical pressure, and I found myself on the floor.

It was now Katie's turn. Apparently, while I was being coached, Katie had opened herself up to the Spirit, as well. Both men and women had surrounded her, and my huddle transferred to her. Soon enough, she was on the floor, too.

"These two young people have the Spirit!" the pastor said, turning to the congregation. He walked back to the front. The band continued with their song.

Trying to clear my eyes, I looked around. Katie was still on the ground, but she was attentive. Andrea was off to the side, looking on with a blank expression. I could only imagine what she was thinking.

After church services, some time later, we all met back at the Recluse. "So, you guys received the Spirit tonight?" Bob said enthusiastically as he entered the shed.

"I think so." I said, Katie affirming the same.

"You think so? That's not something you can guess happened."

"Well, I know what happened tonight was real, 'cause I felt it, but I didn't speak in tongues."

"Me, too." Katie said. She and I had spent the ride back to the Recluse discussing what had happened, but Andrea remained silent. It seemed to Katie and me that we had the same experience. We both had tried the best we could to let the Spirit "take over," but it didn't work. However, we both had one of the most emotional nights we had ever experienced, so we were convinced that the Spirit had done something.

"Why couldn't we speak in tongues?" Katie asked.

"Did you have faith?" Bob asked us.

"As much as I could summon!" Katie said.

"I've gotta tell ya, man," I started, "I've had more faith in the last week than I've ever had. My parents raised me to be a good person and to believe in and pray to God, but you guys are different. I've done the church stuff. I've prayed. My parents are good people. The difference I see between you guys and the world that I'm used to living in is you guys don't say you're Christians; you show that you are. That ten minute conversation you and I had the other day, Bob—you know, the one about the love and justice of God—helped me to understand God more than I ever had. Ten minutes versus seventeen years! What am I to do with that? Did I have faith tonight, when a crowd of people I didn't know were praying for me and touching me? Absolutely."

"Wow," Bob said quietly. "I didn't know our conversation had that much of an impact on you."

"I couldn't sleep that night because of it."

"To tell you the truth, bro, it's probably the only Bible discussion I could ever lead."

"What do you mean by that?" I asked Bob. He seemed honored and humbled at the same time.

"Well, I've heard people use the 'Jesus died for my sins' line so much to justify living a sinful life that I had to learn how to combat it." Bob paused, looking like he was trying to remember something. "Truthfully, that's how I used to live. That was until I came face to face with the justice of God myself. Then I spent a lot of time trying to understand it. I asked pastors. I studied the Scriptures. Now, I feel like it's my duty to help people understand the love and justice of God before they regret justifying sin. You know what I mean?"

I nodded. "Well, it's a good subject to be versed in. Excuse the pun."

"So, you both had faith tonight?" Mick asked, bringing the conversation back. "You invited the Spirit into your lives, but you didn't speak in tongues? Have you been saved before?"

"I don't know," Katie said.

"I have," I said. "I was saved when I was in sixth grade."

"How do you know you were saved?" Bob asked.

"Well, I asked Jesus to come into my heart and forgive my sins."

"That's all well and good, but did you know that's not how you know you're saved? You know you're saved when you speak in tongues," Mick said.

"What? The youth pastor was so excited that night, and so were my friends and I. I went home feeling like a burden had been lifted. I was pretty sure, man."

"I know the feeling, and I understand, but speaking in tongues is like cashing the check and seeing the balance, you know?"

"I never thought about that. No one ever taught me that."

"Have you ever been baptized in water?" Mick asked.

"Yeah. When I was a baby," I said.

"I've never been baptized before," Katie said somberly. "I've always wanted to, though."

"Well, that's probably why you two couldn't speak in tongues tonight!" Bob said. "Were you completely covered in water, Lance?"

"No. The way my parents' church baptizes is by sprinkling."

"You two have to get dunked soon, man!" Mick blurted.

"What's the big deal?" I asked.

"You can't get the Holy Spirit until you're properly baptized." Bob said, Mick affirming with a nod.

"I guess this is serious stuff. If I can know for sure and have what you guys have, I'm willing to do whatever I have to do." I said.

"Me too," Katie added.

"I'll call the pastor tomorrow to see when we can do it," Bob said, beaming.

The Feeding Trough

Saturday, July 19, 2003; West Tennessee

"What's that for?" my mother asked early the next Saturday afternoon, nodding at the bag of clothing. "Swimming?"

"Well, no," I started, not knowing how she would react.

It was sometimes difficult for my mother and me to get into deep conversations. She was very careful not to seem like she was judging me, though she had every good reason to do so. She was my mother. She had the right to tell me what to do and what not to do. Instead, she gave me freedom to express myself through my actions with very few limitations. She was the best mother I ever could have asked for. I knew my mother knew, or at least suspected, of some of my worst teenage decisions. I wasn't as smart as I thought I was.

I was glad and nervous at the same time to tell her that I was making a religious decision on my own, the first since my impressionable tween state. I was glad, because I knew it would tell her that I was moving away from the bad influences in my life. I was nervous, because I was afraid it would seem as though I was rejecting my roots and the fundamentals she had taught me. Yes, I had spent a lot of time with the Baptists in the past, but none of that stuff really replaced or challenged what my family had taught me. She had a Catholic background, and I was baptized as a Lutheran. Now, I was leaving the house to "replace" what she had done for me when I was a helpless child, completely dependent on her decisions and care. How would she react? "Katie and I are actually getting baptized today," I told her.

"Oh," she said before a few seconds of silence. "You've already been baptized."

"I know, but I want to do this, having made the decision to do it myself. I was just a baby when you had me baptized. I want this to be something between God and me, something I choose to do," I said, putting the weight of meaning on my words.

"I know you've been hanging out with those guys for a while, but do you know what you're getting yourself into?"

"These guys are the real deal, and if it means that I'm going to be more like them, I don't think you have anything to worry about." I said, trying to reassure her.

"You know I let you make your own decisions."

"Thanks," I said, putting more meaning in the way I looked at her than on my words. I hugged her and kissed her on the cheek. "Katie's waiting. Love you."

"Love you, too. Be careful." Every time I left the house, she always told me to be careful.

"I will."

Katie and I pulled up to the church at 2:00 pm, just on time. "You ready for this?" I asked her.

"Yeah! Let's do it."

We gathered our bags and made our way into the church building we hadn't been in since the Tuesday night's "huddles." Pastor John met us at the door, and then he led us through the back halls into a big room with a livestock trough on the floor with a hose filling it up with water.

"These are the two that are going to be baptized today," Pastor John announced to the ten or so people who had come to witness the occasion. Bob, Kemp, and Mick could not be there.

"Praise the Lord." "Hallelujah." "Thank you, Jesus," came the replies.

Katie and I had worn the clothes we would get wet in to the church, so we were ready to get baptized as soon as we shook some hands. Katie was first. Once the hose was finished filling up the "baptistery," she sat down in it. The pastor told Katie what he was going to do, and he instructed her on posture and how to plug her nose.

"Katie," the pastor started, much louder than he had previously been talking. "I baptize you in the name of Jesus Christ." Then he dunked her.

I didn't know what to expect next. The guys said that this was how to get the Holy Spirit. What did that mean? How would we know? Would Katie speak in tongues right then and there? The pastor lifted her torso out of the water, and Katie took a breath, wiping the water from her eyes. There was silence as we all waited for Katie's reaction. Standing up, she gave us a big smile.

"That feels great!" she said genuinely.

What was everyone waiting for? Something bigger?

"That's the Holy Spirit! Congratulations, Katie," Pastor John said, putting a hand on her shoulder.

"Praise the Lord." "Hallelujah." "Thank you, Jesus."

"Your turn, son," the pastor said, looking at me.

I got in the trough just as Katie did.

"You know what to do, and you know what I'm going to do?"

"Yes, sir," I affirmed.

"Lance, I baptize you in the name of Jesus Christ," the pastor said with the same exuberance as he did when he dunked Katie. I held my breath and nose, and then he dunked me.

With my head coming out of the water, I opened myself up to the Spirit. *God, do what you've gotta do*, I silently prayed. *Send me your Holy Spirit.* I sat up in the water, wiped away the water from my eyes, and held my eyes closed for a few more seconds. I breathed out heavily. Was it possible to flex your faith? Was it possible to transfer your body's energy to a spiritual quality? I didn't know, but I tried, anyway. Silence. Just like with Katie, people were looking and waiting. I opened my eyes and smiled.

"Praise the Lord." "Hallelujah." "Thank you, Jesus."

Could I say with Katie that I felt great? Yes, but I was also disappointed. Was I disappointed in God? I knew that wouldn't be right, so I found other things to be disappointed in. Did I still lack the required faith? I felt that if I supplied more faith to God, then it would start to hurt. Was I less sincere than the people around me, people who had spoken in tongues before my very eyes just a few nights prior? I had a lot of questions, but it was true that it felt good to show God and my friends that I had faith, whether or not it was enough.

How Do You Know?

Monday, July 21, 2003; Henderson, Tennessee

A couple of days later, Devin was on grill, and I was on chicken duty. "Guess what I did this weekend," I demanded when we both had a chance to talk after our individual breaks.

"You got a job testing out video games?" he said sarcastically.

"Close. I got baptized!"

"Oh, wow!" He responded with enthusiasm. "When and where?"

"Saturday afternoon at the Beacon Apostolic Church."

At that, it seemed a bit of Devin's enthusiasm was replaced with curiosity, and maybe even some concern. "What did you get baptized for?" he asked.

"Well, I had already been baptized as a baby before, but my friends told me that you need to be completely dunked in water to be baptized."

"That's right," Devin added.

I continued. "I was saved when I was in the sixth grade with my friend Derek. He got baptized a little bit later, but

I never did. My friends told me that you've got to speak in tongues before you even know you're saved. So, last week, I went to church with them, and I tried to get the Holy Spirit, but it didn't work. It wasn't until later that they told me I had to get baptized in order to get the Holy Spirit."

"Interesting. So, did you get the Holy Spirit?" Devin asked.

"After church on Tuesday, I knew that I felt great and all, but my friends said that you know when you get the Holy Spirit. I haven't spoken in tongues yet if that's what you're asking. I just need to have a bit more faith. I know it will come. We've got church again tomorrow, so it might happen then."

"I'm sure this past week has been really special for you," Devin said sincerely.

"It really has been. I haven't told a lot of people about my baptism, but I wanted to share it with you."

"That means a lot," Devin said. "I've got a question, though."

"Sure. What is it?"

"What Scriptures did your friends use to tell you all of that?"

"What do you mean?" I asked.

"You know last week when you and I talked about bacon and the Law of Moses? Do you still believe what you learned?"

"Of course I do," I responded.

"Why are you convinced that the Law of Moses is obsolete?" Devin asked.

"Because that's what the Bible says."

"How do you know?" Devin asked, emphasizing that last word.

"Because you showed it to me in the Bible."

"That's what I was hoping you would say. I don't want you to ever think I was just teaching you some church doctrine. I wanted to teach you what the Bible says. So, that's what I mean when I ask what Scriptures they shared with you to convince you about baptism, salvation, tongues, and the Holy Spirit."

"Oh," I responded, trying to think back. After a few seconds, I responded, "You know, I don't recall a single one. I was thinking last week that you were the first person to ever open the Bible to answer a need in my life. As far as I can remember, these guys didn't even mention a single verse. But I know they were speaking from experience. They might not know exactly where the Bible says it, but that's apparently how they knew they were saved and all that."

"I'm sure your friends meant well, and their experiences are also special to them. If it's all true, though, I would like to learn about it from the Bible. How about you?"

"Yeah, of course. You mean, you don't believe what they said?"

"Not exactly," Devin began, "but if I am to answer your question more fully, you can probably imagine what I would want to do, right?"

"You'd want me to take another dinner break with you."

"You got it, man," Devin said with a nod and a smile. "Could you do me a favor? When will you see your friends next?"

"Tomorrow night at church."

"Will you ask them for those Scriptures tomorrow night? I'd like to see where in the Bible it says all of that."

"Yeah, that sounds good. In fact, I'd like to learn, too."

"A noble desire," Devin affirmed.

"Hey, another thing," I said, getting Devin's attention as he turned toward the grill timer. "My band is playing a show this Saturday. I know you'll really enjoy it, since we're a Christian band."

"What do you mean by Christian band?" Devin asked, looking concerned.

"We sing songs about God and to God. We're a ska band. It's kind of like adding brass instruments, just one brass instrument in our case, to punk music."

"I might have to disappoint you. Sorry, man." Devin responded.

"You have other plans?" I asked him.

"Honestly, no. But I don't fully agree with supporting Christian bands."

"What? That doesn't make any sense. You're a Christian, right?"

"Of course I am, and that's why. But, as you can imagine, before I answer you much further—"

"We would have to take another dinner break together," I finished.

"Exactly. I don't mean to offend, but I take this stuff seriously, and I've got to stay committed to what I believe the Bible to teach. Can you accept that for now?"

"Of course I can. That's what I want to do, too. That means

I want to be as serious about the Bible as you. When can we look over some of these things?"

"How about we wait until after your show? You know I don't work on Sundays. Do you work next Monday?"

"Yep."

"How 'bout then?" Devin asked.

"Sounds good to me, man."

Questioning Authority

Tuesday, July 22, 2003; West Tennessee

The next evening, Katie and I showed up at Beacon Apostolic Church ten minutes before services began.

"Man, it's so great to hear about your baptisms," Mick said as soon as he saw us in the parking lot. "I'm so sorry we couldn't be there."

"That's okay," I said.

"How does it feel?"

"It feels great," Katie said with a smile.

"Yeah, it does," I affirmed. "I don't think I've gotten the Holy Ghost yet, though."

"Like I said, bro, it's not something you think, it's something you know."

"I hope I know sometime soon! About that, man. After church, do you think we can talk?"

"Yeah, no problem. Let's go on in."

The order of operations was the same as the previous Tuesday. After an exciting announcement of the baptisms, the band played for a while, while the audience either sang along, swayed back and forth, moved around, or a combination of the three. Then, after the band cooled down, Pastor John and his wife delivered another sermon, which compared our lives without the Spirit to Moses and the Israelites outside of the Promised Land.

During the altar call at the end of the sermon, a couple responded by going up front for people to lay their hands on them and pray for them. I took that opportunity to retreat inside myself, say a few silent prayers to God, grab hold of all the faith I could muster, and bring it to the surface of my life. After the huddle around the penitent couple, the band started up again, along with the din of the audience. I raised my hands with everyone else. I swayed back and forth. I beckoned the Spirit with all of my being to take hold of me.

Nothing.

Why was God disappointing me so much? *No, that is the wrong thing to think!* What was wrong with me? Why didn't I have enough faith? I was sure that not a single fiber of my body was being left out of that moment. Where was the Spirit? How much more faith did I need?

My concentration broke when I felt Mick's hands on my shoulders. *Here we go again,* I thought. I felt some more hands, which rattled me even more. *This doesn't seem like God to me.* I had always understood God as someone who received anyone who offered himself or herself to him. Why did I have to keep trying and trying before the Spirit moved in any way inside of me? It didn't make sense. Why did I have to be a faithful giant before even being convinced I was saved?

That's it, I thought. I twisted free of the hands all over me, and I ducked out of the huddle. I had to get some air and think without all that racket around me.

A few seconds later, I was in the parking lot, feeling the humid summer air, followed quickly by Katie and Andrea. They must have seen the whole thing.

"What's going on?" Andrea asked.

"I'm disappointed, confused, and frustrated. How do I show more faith to God? If I'm lacking it, how do I get more?"

"You've just got to keep trying, Lance," Katie said in an encouraging voice. "I haven't gotten the Spirit yet, but I'm going to keep trying."

"I have a question for you, Katie," I said, turning to look at her seriously.

"Why do you want to get the Spirit like they have it?" I pointed to the building, which was filled with people that my father would have called "Holy Rollers."

"Because I want to be convinced of my salvation. You know that!"

"Of course. And it all makes sense, right? We have to prove ourselves to God so he can prove himself to us? Here's another question, Katie."

"Go on," she said, seeming a bit less defensive.

"How do you know that that's how you know?"

"What do you mean?"

"I mean this," I began, "I know that these people are sincere, and they are our friends. That's why we trust them. But how do you know what they're saying is the truth? They told us we need to get baptized in order to get the Holy Spirit. Then we need to speak in tongues before we know that God kept his promise to save us. How do you know? Have they ever shown us that in the Bible?"

There was silence for a moment.

"I see your point," Katie said quietly. "No, they haven't, but why shouldn't we trust them?"

Andrea leaned against a car. She was silently observing what was going on between us. Andrea was like that. She was wise beyond her years. She knew when to speak and when to stay silent.

"I'm not saying we shouldn't trust them. Again, they're our friends. The other day, my friend Devin and I started talking about a Bible subject. He did something for me that no one had ever done before. He allowed the Bible to answer the questions. Instead of telling me what to believe, he turned pages and had me read it for myself. It was then that I tried to remember when any of our 'friends' have done that for us."

"So, you're saying we shouldn't believe Bob, Mick, and Kemp?"

"That's not what I'm saying!" I said with a raised voice. *That was harsh.* I paused. "I just want to read it for myself, and I was hoping you would, too," I said a little bit calmer.

I saw a couple of people approaching from behind Katie. Mick and Kemp.

"What's up, guys?" Mick asked.

I sighed. These guys already thought I didn't have enough faith. How would it look to them if I started asking questions and asking for proof? There was nothing I could do at that point. It was unavoidable.

"Mick," I started, "I've got questions."

"About what?" Mick asked, cocking his head a bit.

"About all this." I motioned toward the building. "I'm

going to ask you like I asked Katie. How do you know that that's how you know? You said that we can't know that we're saved until we speak in tongues. How do you know that? Where does it say that in the Bible?"

"Somewhere in the book of Acts. I'm not really good at quoting Scripture like the pastor is. Don't worry, bro; it's in there, and I know he knows. Let's go back in. We can talk to him after services. Would that make you feel better?"

I had imagined this going down a lot easier. I imagined us all hanging out later that night, like we normally did. I would then casually ask them to show me the passages. Now, I was flustered. Not only that, but my friends also didn't know how to back up what they had been saying. I didn't want to get more people involved. Enough people already doubted my faith. But my desire to read it for myself outweighed my desire for self preservation.

"It would make me feel better to read it for myself, but I don't want to go back in there right now. I like the music and all, but it's just really hard for me to focus on important things around everyone trying to yell over the music." I turned to Andrea and Katie. "I'll hang out out here. You guys go back in and enjoy the service."

"No," Katie said. "We'll wait out here with you."

"You sure?"

"Yeah. Let's go next door and get something to drink, though," Katie suggested, pointing to the gas station next to the church.

"We'll be out here when you finish," I said to Mick and Kemp.

"Alright, bro. We'll bring Pastor John out here as soon as

we can," Mick said. Then they both went back into the church.

An hour later, Katie, Andrea, and I were all sitting on the trunk of my car, finishing our soft drinks. We could tell that the main service had finished, because people started coming out to their cars. Many people, however, lingered inside the church. Fifteen minutes later, Mick and Kemp were leading Pastor John, Bob, and another man to where we sat.

"Mick says you've got some questions, Lance," Pastor John said with a smile.

"Yes, sir. I do. I want to thank you again for helping Katie and me with our baptisms the other day."

"It was my pleasure, son," the pastor said, inclining his head.

"Now, I don't mean to seem negative or to sound like I'm doubting what you and my friends say," I continued. "I've just really been interested in reading in the Bible for myself the things that I've been taught about baptism, tongues, and salvation. Is that okay?" I asked, looking for an indication that I hadn't asked for too much.

"There's nothing wrong with reading your own Bible to get answers to your questions, son. I presume you're looking for the connection between receiving the Holy Ghost and speaking in tongues as a sign for salvation. Is that right?"

"Yes, sir."

"I don't have my Bible with me. It's still at the podium, but I know the passages are Mark 16:15-17 and Acts 2:38. Do you want me to go get my Bible, so you can see it for yourself?"

My impromptu Bible study with Devin just over a week before made me hungry to learn more, and Devin had convinced me that I could do it on my own. I was anxious to look at these Scriptures for myself, but I didn't want to spend anymore time in that parking lot, especially with Pastor John. He had a demeanor about him that meant well, but came off as judgmental if you were not completely converted to his ways. Though I had spent much of the past few years shrugging off anything that someone thought of me, I really didn't want to seem like a defiant teenager to the pastor. I respected the man. He had baptized me just a few days prior, but I really felt pressured having Pastor John right in front of me. "Can I just write them down and look at them at home?" I asked.

"I suppose I couldn't stop you from doing so," he said with a grin.

I dug into my pocket and found the receipt from the gas station. "Do you have a pen?"

"Yes." He fished inside his suit coat, handed me a fancy pen, and told me the passages again. "You got it?" He looked at me over the top of his glasses.

"Yes, sir." I gave the pen back to the pastor.

Thirty minutes later, I was dropping Katie and Andrea off at the Recluse.

"You sure you don't want to hang?" Katie asked.

"Yeah, but thanks. I've got to work this out on my own pretty soon. Have a good night, ladies."

"Thanks for the ride," Andrea said.

I went straight home. After getting settled into my bedroom, I once again pulled out the leather-cased, maroon Bible from my nightstand. I looked at the table of contents to find out where Mark was. I found the book, turned to chapter 16, and read verses 15 through 17.

> *And he said to them, "Go into all the world and proclaim the gospel to the whole creation. Whoever believes and is baptized will be saved, but whoever does not believe will be condemned. And these signs will accompany those who believe: in my name they will cast out demons; they will speak in new tongues."*

All three were there in the same passage: baptism, salvation, and tongues. I got out a notepad and marked down the observations I made. On the first line, I wrote, "Mark 16:15-17—Baptism, salvation, and tongues connected." Next, I found the second passage, which was Acts 2:38.

> *And Peter said to them, "Repent and be baptized every one of you in the name of Jesus Christ for the forgiveness of your sins, and you will receive the gift of the Holy Spirit."*

There it was again. Forgiveness of sins was definitely part of salvation. I wrote on the second line of the notepad, "Acts 2:38—Baptism, forgiveness of sins, and the Holy Spirit connected." What were these verses teaching me? *I see the connections—baptism, salvation, Holy Spirit, tongues—but how do the pieces fit together?* I saw how my friends at the Apostolic Church put the pieces together, but that was their interpretation. *We're all entitled to our own interpretation*, I thought. *But what is mine?* I didn't have one yet. Maybe Devin could help.

Warning and News

I had to work the following day. I was on dining duty, and Tina was stationed next to me on drive thru. Between rushes of customers, I said to Tina, "I looked up that passage about bacon."

"You did? Did you find what I told you?" she asked.

"Yeah, I did. But that's one of the Old Testament laws. We're not under that anymore, since Christ did away with it."

"Who told you that?"

"Last week, when we were on break together, Devin showed it to me in the Bible."

"Devin? You're letting Devin teach you what the Bible says?" she said with a bit of disbelief and sarcasm in her voice.

"Yeah, what's wrong with that?" I said, confused.

"Devin's a nice guy and all, and we like working with him, but don't you know that his church is a cult?"

"What? What do you mean? Do they brainwash people?" I chuckled with my own disbelief and sarcasm.

"Maybe. I don't know. What I do know is they think you and I are going to hell."

"No way, Tina. How do you know?"

"His church teaches that they're the only 'true' church," Tina began, putting quotation marks in the air when she said the word *true*. "They think all other churches are going to hell."

"Did Devin tell you that?" I asked, starting to get a little upset. Was I upset with Tina? Maybe. If anything, she was dissing my friend. But, if she was telling the truth, I felt quite justified to be upset with Devin.

"No. He didn't have to. I've heard many other people say that, including members of his church."

"Well, he and I are supposed to study the Bible again on break on Monday. I'll talk to him about it then."

"You want my advice?" Tina asked. "Call it off. You're asking for trouble."

"Look," I began. "I see what you're saying, so I'll be careful. But Devin's my friend, and I have no reason to think he'll try to brainwash me. Plus, when we looked at the Bible together last week, he did something for me that no one else has been willing or able to do. He showed me what the Bible says, and he didn't want me to believe anything he said until he was convinced I saw it in the Bible for myself."

"That sounds noble," Tina said. "Just be careful, and make sure you're making your own decisions."

As if on dramatic cue, the next wave of customers started

to come in, making any further conversation with Tina impossible.

After work, I drove by Katie's house to see that the light in the Recluse was on. When I walked in, I saw the whole crew there, including Andrea. "Hey, dudes and dudettes. What's up?" I then noticed how upset Katie seemed. "What's wrong, Katie?"

"Ask Bob."

I looked at Bob, and he gave Katie an apologetic look. "What's going on, man?"

"He wants to go to college. That's what's up," Katie said.

"Good for him," I said. "What's wrong with that?" Then it hit me. "Wait, what does that mean for the band?"

"You've got it, bro," Mick said.

"Say something, Bob." I pleaded.

"Yeah, Lance. I know we've been having a lot of fun, but I just don't see much of a future in all of this." He motioned to all the instruments in the back of the Recluse. "I've been wanting to go to college for several years, but money's always been the issue. My grandfather told me over the weekend that if I enroll in the fall, he'll pay for it all. It's taken me until today to make a decision. So, at the beginning of next month, I'll be off to become a college boy. I know that's not fair to you all, but I also need to be fair to myself and my family."

"Wow." I said. "I can't blame you, but isn't there a way around it? Can't you still continue to do music and travel to us on the weekends?"

"Nah, bro. I wouldn't be able to take the music seriously, and that wouldn't be fair to you guys. Plus, there's no way I could guarantee to be here every weekend."

Kemp spoke up. "Truthfully, guys, this gives me an out."

We all looked at him.

"My family's also been pressuring me to get a better job, something more, 'permanent,' as they say." There were those air quotes again. "To tell you the truth, I'd like something like that, too, but I knew it was impossible to do that and No Hit Wonder, too."

"So, that's it, huh?" I asked. That was the end of my dream. I was finally part of a band of talented musicians who shared my vision, and it was over before it got very far at all. For the second time in the same evening, I was in an emotional dilemma. I couldn't be upset with Bob or Kemp. They both had every right to realign their focuses in life. Regardless, however, I was quite upset. "What about our show this weekend? I've invited all my friends and family."

"It's still on," Bob said. "We'll go out with our guns blazing. How's that sound?" Bob gave me a grin, which beckoned one from me.

"Sounds pretty good," I said, making gun shapes out of my hands and shooting them into the air.

Showtime

Saturday, July 26, 2003; Henderson, Tennessee

After having rehearsed with the band almost all of Thursday, we felt like we were ready for the show on Saturday morning. We had only six songs, but we were convinced it would blow away anyone who came.

Preparing for the performance was bittersweet. I was excited to be involved in my very first rock show, but I couldn't get it out of my mind that, though it was the first, it would also be the last.

I was also nervous about the show. I wasn't nervous until I received confirmation that Lydia was coming, and she was bringing her friend, Abigail, who was visiting her from Texas. Lydia was a girl from school that had consumed my attention for several months during the previous school year. She was a good girl, who inspired me to be a good guy. She was like the guys of No Hit Wonder. She didn't need to cuss and drink to have fun. Her family were Christians, and I tried to be on my best behavior around them. I got along great with her dad, since he also played the guitar. When I heard that Lydia was coming to see us play, I started questioning myself. Did I know the songs well enough? What if I messed the whole thing up? Did I look "rock star" enough to be in a band?

Finally, the time of the performance came. Sure enough, Lydia and Abigail were there. To watch Lydia enjoy the show, anyone could have guessed that we were huge rock stars, and Lydia was our biggest fan. That illusion didn't last long, since only a handful of people showed up.

Without question, I knew I could play music for a living without a single complaint. Though the place wasn't packed, I played like my life depended on it. I soaked in every moment. As a band, we were convinced that "Martyrs of Sinners" was our best, and as every band did, we saved our best song for last. When the time came, I played my bass intro to the song. *This is it*, I thought. *The last song I will play with these guys and girl.* I was surprised when I got emotional. Since I had played the song close to a hundred times, I was able to think about my emotions and surroundings without missing a beat. After the rest of the band came in, Bob began his part.

"They say history repeats itself. How horrific it is true!" came the lyrics.

I remembered my conversation with Bob about what he meant by his lyrics. He had told me, "The idea is that the world is so caught up in sin, that sin is all the world knows." It was the first time I had ever thought of the love and justice of God. "We're taught by the world to be tolerant of sin and to not judge and all that. The world thinks that sin is so important that they would rather die defending their sinful lives, than to look at their lives the way God does and change accordingly." Did that describe me? Had I been living my life defending my actions, or seeking the will of God? According to Bob, at least, you couldn't do both. He was right. The world did focus on tolerance. Tolerance of sin had been so emphasized by my culture that I was almost eighteen years old before I ever considered the justice of God. Bob had told me that sin is punishable by death. When Bob explained it, it had made so much sense. I know that if I mentioned that concept to my peers, they would say something either about the love of God or that Jesus' death on the cross takes care of that, so we had nothing to worry about. If I mentioned that concept to Devin, what would he say? I knew right away. He would ask, "What does the Bible say?" The chorus of the song began.

"Martyrs of sinners, who die so willingly, 'cause they don't see the way that you see!"

Bob had told me that the words of the chorus contrasted the way the world looks at sin and the way that God looks at sin. "We see it as fun, but God sees it as the price of his Son's life." What a thought-provoking concept. I didn't like thinking about it for long, because my conscience would start playing up. Good thing the song was only three minutes long.

When the song was over, Lydia was obviously the most impressed. That made me happy, of course. After unplugging and casing my guitar, I went to her.

"Lance, that was awesome!" Lydia said.

"Thanks. It was a lot of fun."

"This is my friend, Abigail."

"Hello, Miss Texan," I said. "I've heard a lot about you. I hope you can live up to the reputation Lydia's painted." I extended my hand.

"It's good to meet you, too. I'm kind of afraid to ask what she's told you. She's talked a lot about you, too."

Lydia cut in before I could respond. "My parents said they would pick Abigail and me up after they went shopping, so we will have to go soon. I'm going to do what I've been wanting to do for a long time, though." Lydia suddenly looked nervous. I also became nervous. It was always scary when a girl says something like that.

"I want to invite you to church tomorrow."

That's it? I thought. *She's been wanting to do that for a long time?* "Lydia," I said, "how long have we known each other?"

"It's been almost a year."

"Why has it taken you so long to do this? I've always known you to be a church-goer."

"I know, I know. I should have done it sooner. I feel like I can talk to you about almost anything. Anytime I get ready to start a conversation about church, though, I get nervous. I guess I can't ask you to understand, but I'd love for you to come."

Lydia went to the same kind of church Devin went to. I had asked both of them on different occasions if they knew each other, but they both said no. I remembered that Tina warned me to be careful about their church. Did Lydia and her family also think that they were the only ones going to heaven? They had never given me any reason to think they were so narrow-minded. Since I didn't know for sure, and all I knew was what a rumor said, I did what I was good at doing. I gave them the benefit of the doubt.

"I'd be happy to visit your church," I said with a smile.

"Really? Oh, wow!" Lydia exclaimed.

"It wasn't that hard to invite me, was it?"

"No," Lydia admitted, looking down at her feet.

"Are you part of that church, too?" I asked Abigail.

"Yes. I'll be there, too!"

"What time does it start?" I asked Lydia.

"Bible class is at 9:30 am, and regular church starts at 10:30."

"I'll start with regular church."

"Wow. This is great." Lydia said with continued enthusiasm. "We've gotta go now. Great job today! We'll see you tomorrow!"

A Nice Visit

Sunday, July 27, 2003; Henderson, Tennessee

Lydia's dad had previously told me where they went to church. It was close to where I lived, so I knew exactly where it was. When I walked into the front doors of the church, I noticed several things at once. I was not surprised to see many men wearing suits and many women wearing dresses. I didn't have fancy clothes, so I wore the best I had, which were some khaki slacks and a plain, white t-shirt. I was glad to see that several people from my age range were also there. Most of them I had seen at school, and they were not all dressed like the older adults. They helped me feel a bit more comfortable. People were standing around, talking to each other, obviously enjoying their conversations. The foyer was plain. I could see inside the auditorium, and it also was not like any other church I had been to before. There were no stained glass windows. There were no huge banners with crosses or doves on them. There was no organ like in my dad's church or the Baptist Church. There were no amplifiers or drums like in the Apostolic Church. This church apparently didn't put much emphasis on the building. *I wonder why*, I thought. My thoughts were then broken.

"Good morning, sir," a well-dressed elderly man said,

extending his hand. I shook it.

"Good morning."

"It's a blessing to have you here. My name is Gerald. Here's the church bulletin. Are you a Freed-Hardeman student?"

"No, sir. I go to school at Chester County. I graduate next year."

"Oh, I'm sorry to assume," he apologized with his friendly coffee breath. "Is this your first time with us this morning?"

"Yes, sir. It is."

"Again, we are glad to have you. Do you know anyone here?"

"The Sorsky family."

"What a lovely family they are."

In perfect timing, Lydia and Abigail saw me chatting with Mr. Gerald. "Hey, Lance!" Lydia said before thanking Mr. Gerald for welcoming me. She then led me to the rest of her family.

"Hey, buddy!" Mr. Sorsky said, hugging me like he always did. Lydia's family was a really touchy family, which was usually refreshing. "We're just about to begin, so we ought to get seated." He motioned to the pew behind us. "I was really excited when Lydia told me that you were coming. I know what it's like to visit a new church. Feel as relaxed as you can. There's no need to be nervous. When we're finished, ask as many questions as you'd like."

I was glad to have Mr. Sorsky's reassurance. Although I knew I was surrounded by friendly people, I also knew that I was a stranger. He was right. It was nerve-racking to visit a new church. *What should I expect? How much should I participate? How much should I just observe? How will I be judged, regardless of what I do?* We all sat down together.

A man walked up to the microphone up front. "Unto thee, oh Lord, do I lift up my soul..." He was singing. Within seconds, I quickly realized that it wasn't meant to be a solo. The building seemed to erupt with powerful voices. The song was clearly a familiar song to almost everyone inside the auditorium. I felt like I was at a concert. The singing was pure. It was beautiful. From the front to the back, the entire congregation was participating. Some composed perfect harmony. Some of the people were off key. But all were participating, and they didn't seem to care about how good it sounded, yet it sounded very good. There was no wonder why they didn't have a piano up front. They didn't need one!

After a few more songs, none of which were sung by soloists or choirs, but by every member of the church, there was a prayer. Again, I noticed a difference. This prayer was led by one man straight from the heart. The prayers offered in the Lutheran Church always seemed rehearsed and repetitive. I couldn't remember the prayers in the Baptist Church, except for those times the pastor would pray the Sinner's Prayer over the microphone for those responding. The prayers at the Apostolic Church always seemed a bit chaotic to me. They were very sincere prayers, but I could rarely hear them over the outbursts of, "Thank you, Jesus!" "Hallelujah!" and "Amen!" from those in the audience. At Lydia's church, however, the prayer seemed to be the best of all worlds. The crowd participated by bowed heads, closed eyes, and the very occasional and quiet, "Yes, Lord," while the man at the microphone spilled his heart. He praised God, and he petitioned God for help in the lives of all present. He prayed for help in sickness, in spiritual growth, and in church life. He prayed for the local and national government. He prayed for the nation's schools. He prayed for the church leadership. He prayed from the heart, without meaningless repetition, while keeping all reverence toward God. I was impressed, to say the least. I hoped to be able to pray that way some day.

After the prayer, the church sang a few more songs, all of which were filled with joy. Some of the songs were directed toward God, whereas, others had lyrics directed at other Christians, encouraging them to stay faithful and avoid sin.

Then a bald man went to the microphone. "We now take this time to remember our Lord's death." He read a few passages from the Bible and spoke for a few minutes on how much the crucifixion should mean to each person present. He spoke about the cost and cause of the cross. His speech ended in victory, focusing on the resurrection of Jesus. Then he started talking about what he called the Lord's Supper. "We now obey our Lord's words and do this in remembrance of him."

I was somewhat familiar with communion. Though I never remembered ever being present when the Apostolic Church or the Baptist Church participated in it, I had seen my father's church observe it a few times. They did so every now and then, about once a month, and it was always a big deal on the Sundays that they did. Each person who had been confirmed in the Lutheran Church was privileged to participate. They did so by forming lines and walking up to the front of the church. Then the pastor would say something to ten of them at a time and feed them the bread and the wine.

After the man up front said a prayer thanking God for the

cross and the bread, a few more men came up next to him to retrieve plates with bread on them. They started passing them around through the pews.

When I looked around, I saw some people in private prayer. I saw some reading their Bibles. I saw others shushing their children. I saw some looking in the hymnal, reading the words of the song the church had sung last. It was a time of respect and reverence. However, it wasn't the rehearsed reverence I was used to from the Lutheran Church. The people in the pews seemed to connect together as they broke off pieces of the bread and fed themselves. When the tray came to me, since I had not been confirmed yet, I just passed it along.

After the last person was fed and had participated in the eating of the bread, the bald man returned to the microphone and gave thanks over what he called, "the fruit of the vine." His helpers came and passed the next trays in the same fashion as the bread. The worship the church offered was simple, yet refreshing. They didn't seem to be interested in impressing each other. In fact, I got the impression over and over that whoever was at the microphone considered God to be the audience, instead of the people in the pews in front of him.

The bald man returned to the microphone a few minutes later. "Separate and apart from the Lord's Supper, after having focused on God's sacrifice, we take this time to focus on the sacrifice we can make for God."

I was not surprised that the church was taking up money. I did, however, become uncomfortable when I realized I had not anticipated it. Meaning I had not prepared to give, and I didn't have any money in my pockets.

"As we consider our giving this morning," the man continued, "I will read from First Corinthians 16:1-2."

> *Now concerning the collection for the saints: as I directed the churches of Galatia, so you also are to do. On the first day of every week, each of you is to put something aside and store it up, as he may prosper, so that there will be no collecting when I come.*

"Since Paul was instructing the church members to do this, we understand that this passage applies to the local members of the congregation," the bald man said. "If you are visiting with us, please do not feel obligated to give. This is the members' responsibility, and we use the funds for spreading the gospel throughout this community and the world." He then offered a prayer of thanks to God for not only the physical blessings of this world, but also the opportunity to give back.

His words struck me two ways. Everyone around me knew I was a visitor, so no one would judge me when I simply passed the basket. In fact, by the man's words, I was expected to do just that. Secondly, I thought of how righteous that man must be, since he was actually thankful to give up some of his money to the church. That was impressive.

Again, after the collection was taken, the church sang some more songs. *Boy, they sure do love singing.* It didn't bother me, though. I was enjoying every bit of it. I eventually grabbed a hymnal myself and tried to keep up.

Next, a boy my age that I recognized from school got up to the microphone. "The Scripture reading for this morning is First Corinthians 15:1-4." He read the Bible passage as meaningfully as he could.

> *Now I would remind you, brothers, of the gospel I preached to you, which you received, in which you stand, and by which you are being saved, if you hold fast to the word I preached to you—unless you believed in vain. For*

I delivered to you as of first importance what I also received: that Christ died for our sins in accordance with the Scriptures, that he was buried, that he was raised on the third day in accordance with the Scriptures.

After the teenage boy sat down, another man came up to the microphone. *He must be the pastor.* Sure enough, what he had to say was a sermon, and what a sermon it was! He reminded me of Devin. He knew how to make people laugh, but he knew how to treat serious things seriously. He didn't make a single point without first reading that point from the Bible. His message was clear and understandable, and it was all about the death and resurrection of Jesus Christ. I hoped with everything inside of me that Tina's measurement of these people was dead wrong. They didn't seem like a cult, and the guy up in the front didn't seem like the leader of a cult. But wasn't deception a big part of some cults?

After the worship service was over, Lydia looked at me expectedly. "Well?"

"Well, what?"

"What did you think?" she asked.

"I thought it was very nice. This church knows how to sing!"

"Yeah. You'll find that, no matter what congregation you visit."

I spent a few more minutes chatting with Lydia and her family. They continued to tell me how pleased they were that I came to visit. I was pleased for another opportunity to impress Lydia and her family. After the small talk was over, I said my goodbyes and exited the church out of a side door.

That wasn't so bad, I thought to myself. Again, I focused on Tina's warnings. *I'll know more about that when I get to talk to Devin tomorrow.*

The Biblical Body

Monday, July 28, 2003; Henderson, Tennessee

Devin and I were scheduled to come in at the same time the following day. When we both arrived to clock in, Jeanette, the manager on duty, told us, "Everyone needs to read the new notice before work today."

Devin and I both walked over to the board. There was a photo copy from the employee handbook with some highlights. The highlighted text read, "This establishment is determined to provide its employees with an atmosphere that does not discriminate on the basis of gender, race, nationality, age, or religion." The word *religion* was underlined three times. A handwritten note was made under the highlighted text. "Any employee who does not follow this policy is subject to a write-up and/or termination."

"Surely, that's not referring to us, is it?" Devin asked me.

"I'm pretty sure it is, and I think I know why. I told Tina about our Bible study last week. I told her what you showed me, and she didn't seem too happy. I also told her that we had another study planned for this evening. That's still on, right?"

"Sure is, but where are we going to do it now?" Devin

asked.

"We'll have to do it after work somewhere else, I guess. Would that be too late for you?"

"Two facts about me should be able to answer that question," Devin said. "I'm still a bachelor, living on my own, and I'm a college student. What do you think?"

I chuckled. "I'll call my friend Katie. She lives nearby. She's a night owl, too."

"So, what did Tina say?" Devin asked, going back to our previous discussion.

"Well, she gave me a very serious warning about studying with you. Again, she didn't seem happy. That's why I think this all has to do with us. Who else here could be making anyone else uncomfortable about *religion*?" I pointed to the emphasized word on the paper before us.

"I suppose we're the only ones, huh? What did Tina warn you about?"

"She said that your church is a cult, and you think you're the only ones going to heaven. Is that true?"

Devin looked stunned and hurt. "As for your first question, no, we're not a cult," he said. "I suppose you'll have to judge that for yourself, though. Regarding your second question, do you think the Bible can help us with that?"

"I suppose so, Devin," I responded, trying to react with emotion, too. "Look, I know you don't like telling me much without a Bible in your hand, but can you be straight-forward with me on this one? It seems too narrow-minded for me to accept." I stopped trying to hide my frustration. "First, I don't believe you even have to go to church to get to heaven. Secondly, who has the nerve to claim exclusive rights to heaven?"

"There's no way you or I could ever come to a conversation like this without bringing a lot of baggage with us," Devin began with observable control over his cool. "This is obviously important to you, and I think the answer to that question brings meaning to everything you and I have discussed in the past and will discuss in the future. I know you've had a lot of experiences with religious people, and you yourself have claimed how none of them have satisfied you by showing you clear answers in the Bible. Now, are you seriously asking me to do the same and answer you right here on the spot? You know very well what I want to do."

"I see your point," I said thoughtfully. "I know you just want to show me what the Bible says. Who am I to deny you that?"

"I'm very excited that you, my friend, are interested in Bible answers to your excellent questions. I'm serious about finding these answers with you."

"I'm serious, too," I said.

Devin continued, "Then I think the proper question you should be asking is, who are you to deny *yourself* of this opportunity?" Devin paused, apparently giving me the opportunity to protest. I didn't. He was absolutely right. After I raised nothing, he continued. "Tonight, you wanted to discuss what I said last week about Christian bands. I think if we discuss that and your new questions tonight, it might be a bit too much. I think it would be overwhelming for both of us. Should we talk about music tonight, or do you want me to spend time addressing your current question?"

"Actually, I had another thing I wanted to discuss tonight,

too," I said. "I went to church with my friends last Tuesday again, and I did what you said. I asked them for Bible verses on the tongues-salvation thing."

"And were they able to do so?"

"Yes, and I looked them up. I definitely see the connection, but I might need your help understanding it all. You're right, though. If we discussed it all, we wouldn't sleep a wink tonight. Let's talk about your church first. That will make me feel better."

"Okay. That's what we will do. But we had better stop talking about it for now, so we don't get canned."

"Agreed. I'll call Katie on my break to see if we can hang out in the Recluse tonight."

"The Recluse?"

"Yeah. It's a shed behind Katie's house. It's where our band practiced. It doubled as an after-work hangout pad."

"It's where your band *practiced*?" Devin asked.

"Yeah. You know we had a performance this past Saturday?"

"Sure."

"That was our last time together. A couple of the band members couldn't continue, so No Hit Wonder is a thing of the past."

"Wow. Sorry, dude. I hope it was fun while it lasted."

"It was. We're still friends and all, and I'm thinking about starting a new band with Katie. She's a really good singer."

"Nice. I think bands with female singers are pretty cool."

"Yeah, me too. Let's get to work."

During my dinner break later that night, I called Katie.

"Is it cool if I join in?" she asked, when I asked her about using the Recluse for the Bible study after work.

"I'm sure Devin won't mind."

"Great! See you at about 9:30!"

After Devin and I clocked out and went to the parking lot, I asked him, "Do you remember me asking you if you knew Lydia?"

"That girl that you like, right?"

"Yeah. I visited her church yesterday."

"Oh, really?" Devin was enthused. "Which one does she go to?"

"That one on the left of the highway, heading toward Selmer."

"I've never been to Selmer, but I know exactly which one you're talking about," he said. "What did you think about it?"

"Honestly, I was blown away. Everyone was friendly, it was great to see Lydia and her family, and the singing was phenomenal!"

"I expected you would have noticed the music," Devin said with a grin.

"What do you mean? They didn't use music!"

Devin looked confused. "I thought you said there was singing."

"There was."

"And they sang songs?"

"Yeah."

"Isn't that music? There just weren't any instruments," Devin said, making sure I saw the distinction.

"Ah, I see what you're saying. Ok, I guess there was music."

"And you enjoyed it?"

"Like I said, I was blown away."

"Good."

"So, you'll follow me, right?" I asked Devin, motioning toward our vehicles.

"Lead the way!"

When we arrived at the Recluse less than five minutes later, I made proper introductions between Devin and Katie.

"This is a sweet pad!" Devin's eyes were gazing around the inside of the shed. Over the months, we had done everything we could to make the Recluse look like a stereotypical garage band space. In the corner where my bass guitar and amp still rested, you could hardly see the paneled wall through all the posters and album artwork. The most prominent decoration was a flying saucer poster Katie had hung that said, "I Believe," in big, bold letters.

Katie interrupted his room survey. "What's with the cowboy hat?"

"He's from Texas," I said.

"I guess that explains it," Katie said with a giggle.

Devin just stood there with his "proud to be a Texan" look on his face.

"Sorry we have to do this here," I said to Katie. "We were reminded today that if we kept having religious discussions at work, we could lose our job."

"They seriously threatened you?"

"Apparently, it's in the employee handbook," Devin said.

"Last I checked, this is a free country," Katie said.

"Not when someone else is offended," I said, rolling my eyes.

"No bother," Devin said, waving it off. "This is probably a better atmosphere, anyway. Plus, it gives us more than thirty minutes if we need it."

"So, what are we studying about?" Katie started gathering chairs and placing them in a triangle in the center of the room.

"First, Devin and I were going to study about Christian music." I helped Katie situate the chairs. "I also have questions about tongue-speaking."

"You know that I have questions about that, too!" Katie said.

"But," I chimed in, "tonight, Devin's going to show us some stuff about his church."

"What church do you go to?" Katie asked him.

Devin held up his hands. "Before we go much further, we need to establish one thing. Lance, it's not my church. The sign in front of the building where I worship says, 'church of Christ,' for a reason. It's not my church. It's his."

"You're church of Christ?" Katie asked as she and I sat.

"No, I'm not," Devin responded, following suit. "I'm a Christian. That's what I want to show you tonight. Are you ready to see what the Bible says about the church?"

"Let's see it," Katie said. I nodded in agreement.

"Okay." Devin said. "Here goes. The very first time the word *church* is used in the English Bible is in Matthew 16. After spending a lot of time with his disciples, Jesus asked them a couple of questions in verses 13 through 16."

Now when Jesus came into the district of Caesarea Philippi, he asked his disciples, "Who do people say that the Son of Man is?" And they said, "Some say John the Baptist, others say Elijah, and others Jeremiah or one of the prophets." He said to them, "But who do you say that I am?" Simon Peter replied, "You are the Christ, the Son of the living God."

"Peter gave a pretty good answer, didn't he?" Devin asked.

"Yeah. Straightforward guy," I responded.

"Jesus thought so, too. Look here." Devin made sure we could see the Bible he was reading from before he read verses 16 through 18.

And Jesus answered him, "Blessed are you, Simon Bar-Jonah [son of Jonah]! For flesh and blood has not revealed this to you, but my Father who is in heaven. And I tell you, you are Peter, and on this rock I will build my church, and the gates of hell shall not prevail against it.

"Did you see the word *church* in verse 18? What did Jesus say he would do?"

"He said he would build it," I answered.

"And whose church would it be?"

"I suppose, since he said, 'I will build my church,' it would be his, right?"

"Exactly. It would be his and no one else's. Now, the promise in this passage is future tense. He said, 'I will build.' Later in the New Testament, however, after Jesus' resurrection, the church is referred to in the present tense, showing us that Jesus fulfilled his promise. Though the Lord said he would build his church, do you think he was referring to a physical building?"

"Based on the way you asked the question," Katie said, "I don't think so."

"You're right. Let's look at First Peter 2, starting at verse 4. Do you remember, Lance, the questions I told you to ask in order to begin determining the context of a passage?"

"Yep. Who is speaking? Who is that person speaking to?"

"Correct. In this case, it's Peter writing to Christians scattered throughout the first century world."

As you come to him, a living stone rejected by men but in the sight of God chosen and precious, you yourselves like living stones are being built up as a spiritual house.

"You see," Devin said, "Jesus built a spiritual building, and since he is the master builder, we know that his church can exist today. In fact, he promised in Matthew 16 that even the gates of hell, or hades, depending on the translation, can't prevail against it! If we do what they did back then, we will be what they were back then. Peter says that each Christian makes up a single stone in Jesus' building. If you imagine millions of Christians, that would be a pretty big house! And it gets bigger and bigger every time the Lord adds someone to his church."

"So, Christians are automatically part of this church?" I asked.

"Yes. In the New Testament, there was no distinction between the church of Christ and his disciples. For instance, in Acts 8:1, persecution arose against the *church*.

In the next chapter, Acts 9:1, it says that Saul was still threatening the *disciples*. Likewise, in Acts 11:26, the *church* is called *disciples*, who are called *Christians*."

"That makes sense," Katie said. "The church is made up of disciples."

I drummed my fingers on my thigh, still contemplating Devin's point. "You were just talking a lot about Peter. I was always told that he started the church, or, at least, the Catholic Church. Is that true?"

"Sadly," Devin began, "that is a common misconception. The Catholics believe that Peter was the first pope, and therefore, he was the founder of the Catholic Church. However, there is no evidence of that claim anywhere in the Bible. In fact, you cannot even find the words *Catholic* or *pope* in the Bible at all."

"Wow!" Katie said. "I had no idea. I always thought that the Catholic Church was the first church."

"Far from it," Devin said. "About three hundred years from it, actually. The Catholic Church was not an official church until after the Council of Nicaea, which met in 325 A.D. Under that council, the first creed book was written, which helped shape the Catholic Church as it is now."

Based on the expression on Katie's face, I could tell she was just as shocked as I was. How much information in my head was completely false? How much had I blindly accepted in my life without critical thinking?

"I didn't come here to discuss the Catholic Church," Devin continued. "May we keep studying about the church that Jesus established?"

"Yes, please," I said with a nod.

"Thanks," Devin said. "Then a book of the Bible we must

look at is Ephesians." He turned to the book. "It would be best if we had time to read all six chapters tonight, but since I suspect we would all like to see our beds eventually, I'll have to show some highlights. This is what Paul said in the last two verses of the first chapter."

And he [God] put all things under his [Jesus'] feet and gave him as head over all things to the church, which is his body, the fullness of him who fills all in all.

"What is the church called in this passage?"

"Jesus' body," I answered.

"Let me ask you, Lance, how important is your body to you?"

"It's very important!"

"How important, then, do you think Jesus' body is to him?"

"He must think the same, huh?"

"That's the conclusion I've come to, as well," Devin said. "In fact, Acts 20:28 says that God purchased the church with his own blood. The church came with a very hefty price tag, didn't it?"

"Wow. I had no idea the Bible talked about church so much," I admitted.

"Me neither," Katie added.

Devin said, "I know what you mean. It wasn't until a few years ago that I felt the same. Did you know that if you were to count the word *church* in the New Testament, you would find it more than 100 times?"

"No way!" I couldn't believe it.

"Way. Not only that, though, but if you were to count the

times the New Testament refers to the church as the body of Christ, the number would practically double."

Again, I could hardly believe what Devin was saying. If what I was hearing was true, and I had no reason to doubt Devin, then I had seriously underestimated the church. "Show me more." I needed to see what else I was missing.

"Ephesians 4," Devin announced before turning to the chapter. "Look here at verses 5 and 6."

> *one Lord, one faith, one baptism, one God and Father of all, who is over all and through all and in all.*

"Here's my question after this passage: how many Lords should we have?" Devin asked us.

"One," Katie and I said in unison.

"Then wouldn't it make sense for him to have only one body? Before you answer that question, Lance, will you reread the passage, but this time include verse 4?" He handed me the Bible.

> *There is one body...*

I trailed off.

"Keep reading," Devin coached.

> *...and one Spirit—just as you were called to the one hope that belongs to your call—one Lord, one faith, one baptism, one God and Father of all, who is over all and through all and in all.*

"There is one body," I repeated.

"What is the body of Christ?" Devin asked.

"The church of Christ," Katie answered.

Though Katie had no problem, I couldn't answer it right away. I knew the answer. I just had to let it sink in before I did anything. Why did people think that people like Devin were narrow-minded? Because people like Devin simply taught what the Bible said about the church. *The* church. Not *churches*. I had to say it for myself. "The body of Christ is the church, and there is only one body."

"Which means?" Devin beckoned.

"There is only one church," I admitted.

"One day, someone asked me a question, and I've been asking my friends the same question since then. I still keep getting the same answer. The question is, how many churches do you read about in the Bible?"

"Clearly, it's just one," I said. It was so simple. All he did was show me a couple of verses, and something my friends, my family, and I had believed our wholes lives was completely shot down.

"And how many different churches exist in Henderson, Tennessee, alone?" He asked.

"Dozens."

"Is that right? Do you think that is pleasing to the Lord?"

"Well, no," I began. Devin could tell I had more to say. "But I've always been told that we're all on different roads, but we're heading to the same place. At least until now, I have believed it."

"I've heard that, too," Katie added.

"Not all roads lead to the same place, you know. I'll tell you what, Lance, why don't you head south on highway 45, and I'll send Katie east on I-40. Let's see who gets to Nashville first."

"Good point," I surrendered.

"If we saw a person with just one head, but several bodies, would we consider that normal?"

"Of course not."

"Then why should we think it's fine for Jesus to be the head over many different bodies? It's completely unbiblical. Let's look at the next chapter," Devin said. "Starting at verse 22, Paul starts teaching about the relationship between husbands and wives, but verse 32 tells us that he is actually speaking about Christ and the church. Now, read verse 23 for us. I was eager to do so, yet I was afraid of what I was about to learn.

> *For the husband is the head of the wife even as Christ is the head of the church, his body, and is himself its Savior.*

"Again," Devin began, "this verse teaches us that Jesus is the head of the church. How many heads should his body have?"

"Just one," I said.

"So, what does that mean about our Catholic and denominational friends?" Devin asked. "The Catholics point to the pope, and they call him the head of their church. Many denominations also have heads over their churches, heads who are not Jesus. What about that?"

"That's not right," I said. "But doesn't the Bible say we shouldn't judge?"

"That's a good question, but to properly deal with it, we would need another night. But are we really judging? Haven't we simply read what the Bible says? We all just want to do what's right." Devin started turning to a new passage. It was Second Timothy 3:16-17. "Notice this," he said.

> *All Scripture is breathed out by God and profitable for*

teaching, for reproof, for correction, and for training in righteousness, that the man of God may be competent, equipped for every good work.

"Notice that all Scripture can train us in doing what is right. All we have to do is read and follow what is written in black and white in front of us. When we see something that goes against Bible teaching, we should recognize it and avoid it. Is that fair?"

Katie was already nodding.

"Fair enough," I said. "You'll have to excuse me. This has been an eventful couple of weeks for me, religiously speaking. It's all new to me, and if you haven't noticed, I'm a bit on the defensive."

"It's fine, man," Devin reassured. "I was just the same. Are you ready to keep going?"

"Sure."

"Okay. I have one more question about the passage we read a minute ago. Ephesians 5:23 told us that 'Christ is the head of the church, his body, and is himself its Savior.' According to what the Bible says right in front of us, who is it that Jesus saves?"

Earlier this evening, in a small fit of anger, I had told Devin that I didn't believe salvation and church were linked together. Again, my presuppositions were destroyed.

"I had never thought of that," Katie said.

"What does it say?" Devin asked again.

"Jesus is the Savior of the church," I admitted.

"Are you starting to see some things tonight for the first time that go against what our culture is teaching us?"

"Absolutely," I said. "And I don't like it. It just feels narrow-minded. There is only one church that's going to be saved? I know good people in lots of different churches. In fact, I've heard someone pray before, thanking God for the many different churches out there so that we can all have a choice on how to worship him."

"Yes, it sounds narrow-minded to some. Then again, people thought the same about Christ when he was on the earth and was teaching with authority. It doesn't feel right to many, but can I show you what the Bible says concerning those two concepts?"

"How can I say no to that? I'd obviously only be hurting myself. Go for it," I said.

"Alright. The first one is a warning from Jesus himself in Matthew 7:13-14."

> *Enter by the narrow gate. For the gate is wide and the way is easy that leads to destruction, and those who enter by it are many. For the gate is narrow and the way is hard that leads to life, and those who find it are few.*

"Jesus," Devin began, "describes the gate that enters to life as *narrow*, and the amount of people who enter it as *few*. However, *wide* and *many* are used for the alternative. It's so easy to follow the world. Nobody judges you. It's easy to do what everyone else is doing. But we all know it's difficult to stand up for the truth, and it's even harder to follow it. This concept sounds narrow-minded because the path that leads to life is *narrow*."

"You've done it again, Devin," I said, shaking my head. "How do you know so much?"

"Don't give me the credit, man. It's God who is teaching you. There's no wonder why Hebrews 4:12 says, 'For the word of God is living and active, sharper than any two-edged sword, piercing to the division of soul and of spirit, of joints and of marrow, and discerning the thoughts and intentions of the heart.' Here's another passage. Be careful about going off of your feelings. Look at what Proverbs 14:12 warns us about."

There is a way that seems right to a man, but its end is the way to death.

"If only we could spend as much time tonight warning about the dangers of following the heart. But, again, we are here to study about the church, so we will leave that for another day. How 'bout we continue?"

"Yes," Katie said.

"Yep," I agreed. I was determined to keep going. This was the most challenging concept I had ever faced, spiritually speaking, and it was all true, coming straight out of the Bible.

"Good determination. Before we do so, let me ask another question. What does the word *denomination* mean?"

"I don't know," I admitted.

"I know what a denominator is," Katie said. "It's the bottom number in a fraction. It's what numbers are divided into."

"You're definitely on the right track," Devin affirmed. "A denomination is a division from a whole. For instance, if you had a one hundred dollar bill, and you ask a cashier to divide it for you, she would ask your denominational preference: fives, tens, twenties, and so on."

"Makes sense to me," I said.

Devin continued. "The next passage is in First Corinthians 1. The apostle Paul had heard some things about the church meeting in Corinth that were not good. Among their selfishness and sexual sins, they were dividing into different groups. Apparently, the issue of division was so important that the Holy Spirit, through the pen of Paul, decided to deal with that first. Let's read verses 10 through 13.

> *I appeal to you, brothers, by the name of our Lord Jesus Christ, that all of you agree and that there be no divisions among you, but that you be united in the same mind and the same judgment. For it has been reported to me by Chloe's people that there is quarreling among you, my brothers. What I mean is that each one of you says, "I follow Paul," or "I follow Apollos," or "I follow Cephas," or "I follow Christ." Is Christ divided? Was Paul crucified for you? Or were you baptized in the name of Paul?*

"Do you see what was happening? They were dividing over different preachers. They decided to follow men, instead of God. That's exactly what a religious denomination is, isn't it?"

"That's what I've always thought, too," Katie said.

"You have the Presbyterians following the teachings of John Calvin. John Wesley started the Methodist church. The Catholics follow the pope. The Lutherans are named after Martin Luther. On and on it goes. Which one of those churches can you read about in the Bible?"

"None of them," I said. He was exactly right. I was raised in the Lutheran Church, a church started by a man a few hundred years ago. Now that I thought about it in the light of the Bible, it made no sense! Why would anyone want to be part of a religious group that claimed to honor God, but named themselves after a man, who was born almost 1,500 years after Christ?

"If there is a church in existence today that was started by men, is it the church that Jesus established in the first century?" Devin asked.

"It can't be," I said.

"In John 17," Devin began, "we have a long prayer of Jesus Christ recorded for us. In verses 1 through 5, he prays for himself. In verses 6 through 19, he prays for his apostles that would be commanded to teach the gospel to all nations. Starting in verse 20, he prays for those people who believe through the message of the apostles. That's us! Look what Jesus prays concerning all those who claim belief in Christ in verses 21 through 23."

> *that they may all be one, just as you, Father, are in me, and I in you, that they also may be in us, so that the world may believe that you have sent me. The glory that you have given me I have given to them, that they may be one even as we are one, I in them and you in me, that they may become perfectly one, so that the world may know that you sent me and loved them even as you loved me.*

"What does he pray for all believers?"

"That we all be one," I answered. "There's no mistaking it."

"Does the religious world have this type of unity today?" Devin asked.

"Not at all," Katie said. That's the entire reason why I was disgusted with Christianity for so long.

"You're not alone," Devin assured. "Not only do we need to be one in the one body of Christ, but when Paul was exhorting the Corinthian Christians, he told them to be united 'in the same mind,' meaning that they were to teach and believe the same things. In Romans 15:6, the same apostle told the Romans to be united in 'one voice' while glorifying God, meaning they were to worship the same way. Today, the world is excited about new interpretations and new ways of worship. Do you think that's pleasing to the Lord?"

"I've always thought that everyone was entitled to their own interpretation," I answered.

"Is that the truth from the Bible, though?" Devin challenged.

I shrugged.

"I'm thinking of two passages that can help us with that," Devin said. "The first is Hebrews 13:8-9."

> *Jesus Christ is the same yesterday and today and forever. Do not be led away by diverse and strange teachings.*

"Since Jesus Christ is always the same, why would his message change? Imagine a father telling his four children at the same time, 'Go clean your room.' Do you think they are all entitled to their own interpretation as to what he means?"

"Of course not," I said.

"Why would we treat our Heavenly Father any differently? He has given us all the same commandments, and we're told in Romans 2:11 that God does not show partiality. He treats us all the same. Secondly, I'd like to look at Second Timothy 4. In verses 1 and 2, Paul charges Timothy to preach God's word. He was to 'reprove, rebuke, and exhort.' Verses 3 and 4 tell us why.

> *For the time is coming when people will not endure sound teaching, but having itching ears they will accumulate for themselves teachers to suit their own passions, and will turn away from listening to the truth*

and wander off into myths.

"Why do you think divisions started occurring in the church, eventually resulting in recognized denominations?"

"People are selfish," I said.

"I suppose I couldn't have put it clearer," Devin said, nodding. "Yes, Paul warned Timothy to preach the word, because the time was coming, even during the first century, when people would stop listening to the truth and begin gathering around teachers that would teach what their itching ears wanted."

My mind was racing. Not only had Devin shown me exactly everything I needed to see, and at the same time everything I didn't want to see, but I could also see how practical the Bible was. I had been treating the Bible as some sacred, ancient book, which it was, but, as Devin had quoted earlier from Hebrews 4:12, it was also living. It was able to pierce straight into my conscience and expose me for the product of modern culture I was.

"So, what about the church of Christ, Devin?" I asked.

Katie spoke up. "I was just wondering that, too."

Devin answered my question with a question. "Who do you suppose started the Lutheran church?"

"Obviously, Martin Luther," I said, already sensing where he was going.

"Who do you think started the church of Christ?"

"I suppose what I'm supposed to say is *Christ*, right?"

"I'll let you be the judge of that," Devin said. "If you've found this Bible study tonight truthful and helpful, then I assume we can keep studying."

"Absolutely," I said. "You know I still have some hanging questions."

"Good. After a few more studies, you'll be able to look inside the Bible, and look at the church of Christ, and see if we really are that church that Jesus established," Devin assured. I shifted in my seat as he continued.

"By the way, the church in the Bible isn't known by any proper name. It didn't need a proper name. Think about it. There was only one church in the first century. If you lived back then, and someone said, 'I'm a member of the church,' you wouldn't even think to ask, 'Which church?' In the Bible, the one church is known by many phrases, such as the church of God, Acts 20:28; the church of Christ, Romans 16:16; and the body of Christ, Colossians 1:18; to name just a few. Most frequently, however, it's simply referred to as the church or the body. So, from now on, when I refer to the church, unless I say otherwise, I am referring to the church we can read about in the Bible. When you see a sign in front of a building that has those three words, *church of Christ*, that's not necessarily a proper name. That's hopefully a description of the people you'll find assembling in that building. We're not 'Church of Christers.'" Devin made air quotes with his fingers. "We're Christians. Likewise, just because the sign says they are the *church of Christ* doesn't mean they are the church of Christ. You have to compare them to the church that you read about in the Bible." Devin pointed to the book in his hand. "I've got two more questions for you, Lance and Katie."

"Go ahead," I said.

"First question: If I read and follow the Bible correctly, which church do I become part of?"

"Jesus' church," Katie answered.

"Agreed," I said, nodding.

"Right. Now, I want you to think of a denomination. Any denomination. But don't tell me which one."

I expect Katie either thought of the Baptist Church, since her family had roots in it, or the Apostolic Church, since she and I had recently been so involved with it with our friends. I broke the rules and started thinking of three denominations. I thought of the Lutheran Church, since most of my family would have still claimed to be Lutherans. I thought of the Baptist Church that I had attended with Derek so much in the past. I also thought of the Apostolic Church.

"Do you have one in mind?"

Katie and I both nodded.

"You become part of Christ's church by reading and following the Bible, as we all agree. Here's the next question: how do you become a part of the denomination you have in mind?"

There was a silent pause.

"Wow," Katie said. "I don't know, but since we don't read of it in the Bible, I guess you have to find the answer outside of the Bible, huh?" She seemed a bit stunned.

"My point exactly," Devin said.

I stayed silent. Devin was absolutely right, and I'm sure he could tell what I was thinking by my silent expression. My thinking had to change, and it had to do so based on God's word.

Devin stood up. "I have a homework assignment for you two."

"It's summertime. No homework," Katie playfully

protested.

"Don't worry. It won't take long. I want you to keep thinking about that last question, and then read Galatians 1:6-12. Report back to me on it the next time we see each other."

"I suppose that's easy enough," Katie said, smiling.

I grabbed one of the several notebooks and one of the pens in the Recluse to write down the passage. The notebooks were necessary for any strokes of genius that hit us during band practice that had to be recorded right away.

"I'll definitely do it," I said.

"Me, too."

"You'll be the better for it," Devin said with a grin.

"Devin, this was really interesting and helpful," Katie said, standing up. "Thanks, Lance, for introducing me to Devin and bringing your study here. When can we do this again?"

"You're working tomorrow, right?" I asked Devin.

"Yep. 4:30 pm."

"Me, too. Do you want to do the next study tomorrow at the same time, same place?"

"I'll be happy to. Keep in mind, I'm getting married next month. In bachelor speak, that means my free time after work will probably be limited once I'm married."

"Gotcha," I said.

"You're getting married? Congratulations!" Katie said.

After parting ways with Katie and Devin, I took my time driving home. *Only one church. Jesus is the Savior of the body. Where am I? Am I in the body?* My mind was reeling, as I had so many questions. Since I started working at the restaurant, my mother was used to having me come home late, since I would frequently stop at a friend's house after work, or the Recluse more recently. She usually went to bed at 9:00 in the evening, anyway. By the time I was on my way home on this particular evening, it was nearing midnight. The only reason why I applied any speed to my trek home was so I could do my "homework." I had to see what that Bible passage said to find out how it related to the church.

What would Mom think? She was raised Catholic, but converted to Lutheranism for my dad's sake. I was raised Lutheran, I attended the Baptist Church, and I had recently been baptized as an Apostolic. Now, I was learning that all of those churches were man-made. Surely, I would look quite unstable if I switched persuasions again. I was, however, searching for truth, and I was following it wherever it led me. I had to make the decision for myself.

My mind raced while I drove home. Taking twice as long as normal to get there, I finally pulled into the driveway. I made straight for the nightstand. I pulled the note out of my pocket. "Galatians 1:6-12." I looked at the table of contents to save time. Page 972.

> *I am astonished that you are so quickly deserting him who called you in the grace of Christ and are turning to a different gospel— not that there is another one, but there are some who trouble you and want to distort the gospel of Christ. But even if we or an angel from heaven should preach to you a gospel contrary to the one we preached to you, let him be accursed. As we have said before, so now I say again: If anyone is preaching to you a gospel contrary to the one you received, let him be*

accursed. For am I now seeking the approval of man, or of God? Or am I trying to please man? If I were still trying to please man, I would not be a servant of Christ. For I would have you know, brothers, that the gospel that was preached by me is not man's gospel. For I did not receive it from any man, nor was I taught it, but I received it through a revelation of Jesus Christ.

Vain Worship

Tuesday, July 29, 2003; Henderson, Tennessee

Before we got off work, Devin and I paid for and scooped our own milkshakes from the restaurant, making an extra one for Katie. We didn't dare discuss the Bible at work, though I was very anxious to discuss the homework with Devin. Finally, with delicious shakes in hand, we made our way to the Recluse.

"I did my homework," I said as we sat down in the shed.

"Me, too," Katie said, taking her first slurps.

"And what did you two learn?" Devin asked.

"God takes his message very seriously," I said.

"And that we shouldn't be listening to any other messages," Katie added.

"Precisely," Devin said with a nod. "The reason why I put you two on that is because of something you said last night, Lance. You said that you believed that everyone is entitled to their own interpretation. We read a couple of passages that dealt with that, didn't we?"

Katie and I nodded.

"Well, the warning in Galatians 1 should help us even

further. To teach anything contrary to the message of God is to cause you and your listener to be accursed by God." Devin used the ribbon in his Bible to quickly turn to a passage. It was Second Peter 1:19-21. "Will you read this for us, Lance?"

> *And we have something more sure, the prophetic word, to which you will do well to pay attention as to a lamp shining in a dark place, until the day dawns and the morning star rises in your hearts, knowing this first of all, that no prophecy of Scripture comes from someone's own interpretation. For no prophecy was ever produced by the will of man, but men spoke from God as they were carried along by the Holy Spirit.*

"Certainly," Devin began, accepting the Bible back from me, "interpretation is necessary to understand any communication. However, when it comes to the word of God, we are told over and over in Scripture that God means what he says, and we have no right to twist or teach otherwise."

"Fair enough," I said. "Devin, you have taught me more about the Bible in the past couple of weeks than I have ever learned. I can't speak for Katie, but you have also shown me how practical the Bible is. I trust you to teach the truth."

Katie agreed. "I'm here again because of how much I learned last night. Lance also says you can help us with what the Bible says about tongues. I didn't really question it until Lance made me question it the other night."

"I appreciate the trust, you two," Devin said with a genuine smile. "However, all I am doing is showing you what the Bible says." Devin pointed emphatically to the book in his hand. "All people can learn this stuff if they simply read the Scriptures. I'm not the authority. God is.

Is that clear?"

It certainly was. My respect for Devin was growing by the minute. When any other man would have eaten up the glory and praise by men, Devin humbly and happily stood behind the Bible, allowing its author to receive all the glory. I assumed he and Paul had something in common. I had read during my homework assignment:

> *For am I now seeking the approval of man, or of God? Or am I trying to please man? If I were still trying to please man, I would not be a servant of Christ. For I would have you know, brothers, that the gospel that was preached by me is not man's gospel.*

During break from work that night, when I called Katie to confirm our meeting after work, I had informed her what we were planning on studying that night. We were there to study why the church of Christ didn't use instruments in their worship. If we had time, we would also study speaking in tongues. Finishing my milkshake and turning to her, I asked, "Are you ready?"

"Absolutely! Preach it, Reverend!" Katie said to Devin with a giggle.

"Whoa, whoa whoa!" Devin said, pulling invisible horse reigns. "I might be sanctified by the blood of Christ, but I'm not God!"

"What do you mean?" I asked, raising my eyebrows.

"There's only one place in the Bible that you can find the word *reverend*, and it's attributed to God alone. Don't ever call someone by the title *Reverend*, unless you're talking to God," Devin gently instructed us, looking at Katie.

"We called my pastor *Reverend* all the time growing up," Katie said.

"There are a lot of traditions that churches teach that originate with man and not God, such as giving people titles like *Reverend*. Jesus dealt with the Pharisees of the first century, a group of people who were notorious for following the traditions of their religious leaders." Devin turned to Mark 7:6-9. "Look what he told them here."

> *And he said to them, "Well did Isaiah prophesy of you hypocrites, as it is written, 'This people honors me with their lips, but their heart is far from me; in vain do they worship me, teaching as doctrines the commandments of men.' You leave the commandment of God and hold to the tradition of men." And he said to them, "You have a fine way of rejecting the commandment of God in order to establish your tradition!"*

"Jesus really knew how to put people in their place, didn't he?" I asked.

"For sure," Devin answered. "They were rejecting what God had said in order to follow the traditions of men. For that, Jesus called them hypocrites! They went around with a 'holier than thou' demeanor, yet they didn't practice what they preached! One of the traditions that people follow without question today is calling their preacher *Reverend*. Be careful what you do in the name of God. It might not be by God's authority at all. I'm glad this came up, because this point is completely related to the subject of music. In the passage we just read, Jesus contrasted two teachings: the traditions of men and the commandments of God, right?"

"Yes," I said.

After getting permission to do so, Devin grabbed the notebook and pen on the floor. He made two columns on a piece of paper. The left one was labelled "Commandment of God," and the other was "Traditions of Men." Then he asked us, "What will Jesus call us if we follow whatever lands in this second column?"

"Hypocrites," Katie answered.

Then Devin wrote, "Hypocritical" above "Traditions of Men." He continued, "Also, in Mark 7:7, Jesus said that if you honor God with your lips, but your heart isn't in it, it is vain worship, right?"

"Yes," Katie agreed.

"Which would mean that the worship is useless or empty," Devin continued. He then wrote "Vanity" at the bottom of the second column. Afterward, he turned to and read Jesus' words in John 4:23-24.

> But the hour is coming, and is now here, when the true worshipers will worship the Father in spirit and truth, for the Father is seeking such people to worship him. God is spirit, and those who worship him must worship in spirit and truth.

"Should we strive to be true worshipers or false worshipers?" Devin asked.

"True, of course," I answered.

"Right you are," Devin said. Then he wrote "Spirit and Truth" above "Commandments of God." Then he turned to John 17. Before reading verse 17, Devin said, "Jesus is praying to the Father on this occasion."

> Sanctify them in the truth; your word is truth.

"Tell me," Devin said. "What does Jesus consider to be truth?"

"God's word," Katie said without hesitation.

"Right you are! Therefore, if we are to be true worshipers,

we do what God's word tells us to! Is that fair enough?"

"Fair and simple," I agreed.

Devin then wrote "Biblical" at the bottom of the first column. He said, "Before we discuss music, I want to quickly look at the concept of communion." He turned to Matthew 26 and pointed at verse 17. "In the context of the very first Lord's Supper, Jesus and his disciples were eating unleavened bread. In verse 29, Jesus refers to the drink as 'fruit of the vine.' My question is, during communion, if we want to be true worshipers, what two elements must we use?"

"That's easy," Katie said.

"Unleavened bread and fruit of the vine," I said, proving Katie's point.

"I agree," Devin said. "Would it be okay if I used cake and soda next Sunday instead?"

"No way!" Katie blurted.

"Ok, well, what if I used it in addition to the elements mentioned in Matthew 26?"

"That's not right," I said.

"Why not?" Devin asked. Devin was a great teacher. He didn't simply tell us what we needed to know. Asking several open-ended questions that he already knew the answers to, he coached us into finding it out on our own.

"Because the Bible tells us what to use," I said.

"But the Bible doesn't say I *can't* use cake and soda!" Devin protested.

"That's beside the point," Katie said.

"Which is my point exactly," Devin said with a smile. "If

the Bible were to take the time to list everything we are not supposed to use, it would fill a whole library on the subject of communion alone! Jesus knew that giving us specifics was enough. Where specifics are mentioned, we have no freedom to add to or take away from what has been given."

"That makes sense to me," I said.

"Me, too," Katie said, nodding.

Devin then wrote, "Unleavened Bread and Fruit of the Vine" under the "Commandments of God" column. He also wrote "Cake and soda" under the "Traditions of Men" column. "Now that we've established this," Devin said, "I want us to look at the biblical way God wants us to worship him in song." Devin turned to Ephesians 5:18-19 and read.

> *And do not get drunk with wine, for that is debauchery, but be filled with the Spirit, addressing one another in psalms and hymns and spiritual songs, singing and making melody to the Lord with all your heart.*

"What kind of music does the Bible tell us to use in this passage?"

"Singing," Katie and I said in unison.

"Okay. Next, we'll look at James 5:13."

> *Is anyone among you suffering? Let him pray. Is anyone cheerful? Let him sing praise.*

"What kind of music does God desire for New Testament praise?"

"Singing."

"Right," Devin said with a nod. "And if we were to look at all the passages in the New Testament that give us either commandments or examples of such, it would always say *sing*. Not once is an instrument of music mentioned in the context of Christian worship or praise in the New Testament."

"What about David?" I asked. "Didn't he play the harp?"

"Yes, he absolutely did," Devin said. "But he also sacrificed bulls and goats for his sins. Should we do that, too?" Devin had me there. "He also refrained from eating bacon, too. What did you and I study about following only one part of the Law?"

Just two weeks earlier, Devin and I had studied about the difference between the Old and New Testament laws. We saw in the Scriptures that anyone who did not follow the entire Law of Moses was cursed, and if he wanted to follow one law, he had to follow them all. Although the information was still fresh on my memory, I was already going against what the Bible had taught me. Truthfully, I was just looking for an excuse to hold on to my beliefs. I could see where Devin's teachings were heading, and I knew they would be biblical. As I was quickly learning, it is easier to accept what you've always been taught without question, than to put forth the effort to learn and accept the truth. "Good point," I finally admitted.

"I see what you're saying, Devin," Katie chimed in. "Just like communion, since God has given us specifics about musical praise, we've got to respect it by doing what it says without adding or taking away from it, right?"

"That's exactly what I'm trying to say! There are a few examples in the Bible where someone has gone beyond what was commanded and was punished accordingly. One of the clearest examples is in Leviticus 10:1-2. There were some priests under the old covenant, who added an element of worship that was not commanded. Devin read it, emphasizing a phrase in the middle.

> *Now Nadab and Abihu, the sons of Aaron, each took his*
> *censer and put fire in it and laid incense on it and*
> *offered unauthorized fire before the LORD, which he had*
> *not commanded them. And fire came out from before*
> *the LORD and consumed them, and they died before the*
> *LORD.*

"You see," Devin continued. "They were punished, not because they did the opposite of the direct commandment, but because they added to what God had specified. According to Deuteronomy 4:2, adding to or taking away from God's commandments is the same thing as breaking them. I was sorry to have to decline your invitation to your performance on Saturday, you two, but I now think you might understand why."

"Yeah," Katie said with a depth to her voice.

"When you told me, Lance, that you were in a Christian band that sang about God and to God, I could not support it with all good conscience. The church of the Bible didn't use instruments in their worship, and neither will I. In fact, even history books will tell you that instruments in 'Christian' worship were not added until several hundred years after Christ established his church."

There was no wonder why the church of Christ had such great singing. It was because they had complete resolve to worship God in spirit and in truth, adding no traditions of men. I now had more respect for the church, which I was so quick to insult just a day prior, than I ever had. I spent my whole life in churches that had, at very least, organs in them. I had done so without ever a second thought. I was following the traditions of men without question. What would Jesus have said to me?

> *This [person] honors me with [his] lips, but [his] heart is far from me; in vain [does he] worship me, teaching as doctrines the commandments of men.* Mark 7:6-7.

I was a hypocrite, having wanted to honor God without ever consulting him as to how to do so. If I would have just taken the time, I would have found the commandment,

> *Let the word of Christ dwell in you richly, teaching and admonishing one another in all wisdom, singing psalms and hymns and spiritual songs, with thankfulness in your hearts to God.* Colossians 3:16.

Finally, Devin completed the two columns on the sheet of paper. The left column said, "Spirit and Truth; Commandments of God; Unleavened Bread and Fruit of the Vine; Biblical; Singing." The column on the right side said, "Hypocritical; Traditions of Men; Cake and Soda; Vanity; Instrumental Music."

Katie and I were both, once again, blown away by what we had just learned from God's word. We knew we had one more subject to study that night, so, having finished our milkshakes, we took a short break, and Katie went inside her house to retrieve some water for us each.

Linguistic Fishermen

Tuesday, July 29, 2003; Henderson, Tennessee

"Have you learned anything new so far tonight?" Devin asked as the three of us walked back into the Recluse.

"Sure have!" Katie said.

I was the first to sit back down. I was nervous and anxious about the next hour. "Absolutely," I said. "And ever since I met you, a certain truth about my life has made itself known."

"Oh, yeah? What's that?" Devin asked with raised eyebrows.

"I have no idea what the Bible says." Devin and Katie silently found their seats. Devin was likely giving me the time I needed to either express myself further or let this truth sink in deeper. Katie was unreadable. Finally, I said, "My family has always treated the Bible as something special. We've all accepted the major themes, like creation and that Jesus died for our sins, but I've spent more time in the past couple of weeks with an open Bible than I ever have before." Again, there was silence until Devin broke it.

"Do you know what the world's biggest religion is?" When I just looked at him, waiting for him to answer his own question, he shattered the suspense. "Confusionism. The world is confused for the very same reason you're frustrated right now. They have gone their entire lives believing their church leaders. They're putting their souls in the hands of men. There's no wonder why people criticize 'Christians.'" Devin put quotation marks in the air. "The Bible says that God is not the author of confusion, but of peace, yet what do we see in the 'Christian' world today?" Again, Katie and I left the question hanging in the air.

"I want to show you something" Devin turned to Acts 17:11. "Saul and Barnabas, preachers for Christ, had spent some time in Thessalonica, but their lives were threatened. Going to the next city, they began preaching the same message."

> Now these Jews were more noble than those in Thessalonica; they received the word with all eagerness, examining the Scriptures daily to see if these things were so.

"Why did the Holy Spirit call these people *noble*?" Devin asked.

"They were willing to check the facts before believing the preachers," Katie said, immediately getting Devin's point.

"How much more united the religious world would be today if all who claim Christ would do the same!" Devin exclaimed. "I hope you know that I don't want you to believe a thing I say during these studies, unless you are convinced it is the truth from the Bible."

"Devin, I appreciate your willingness to share the Bible with us," I said genuinely. "I know that is exactly what you're doing, too. You're sharing the *Bible*. All the religious groups I've been involved with have been either traditional ritualistic, happy-go-lucky, or charismatics based on emotion. I'm ready to get serious and finally see what God's word has to say."

"Your openness to God's word will change your life. Just keep that attitude, and you'll see for yourself soon enough," Devin encouraged.

Since the previous night's study on the Bible's definition of the church, I was completely ready for Devin's latest words to become reality. Sure, I had learned a lot, but how much had it *changed* me? Was my life's direction any different than it had been before I had opened the Bible with an open mind? Not really. *God, let it be so. I'm ready*, I silently prayed.

From my wallet, I retrieved the note I had made while looking up the passages on tongues and salvation. While handing it to Devin, I said, "I believe you. The Bible is going to change my life. The entire reason why I looked up these passages is because I wanted to know I was saved. If tongues really is what my friends have told me, then that would change my life. We're all ears, Devin. Show us what it says."

"These are the passages they gave you?"

"Yes. I looked them up myself, and those are my observations."

"Good for you for doing this. You read the passages in context, right?"

I slapped my forehead. "I remember our conversation at the restaurant about context. I had completely forgotten about it when I looked up those verses. I guess I just did what came naturally."

"What's it mean to read in context?" Katie asked.

"It means to understand the things around a passage." Devin answered. "We can quote individual verses all day long, but if we don't read them in context, we will very often misunderstand what the passage means. We've got to read the stuff before and after the verse in question. If possible, we also have to understand the historical context, too—you know, the stuff that was going on in the time and place where it was written."

"Sure. That sounds fair," Katie said with a nod.

"Let's go ahead and read this first passage, and we'll do so in context." After giving me a quick glance, Devin turned to Mark 16. "First, we must realize that the beginning of the chapter tells us that this takes place after Jesus' resurrection. Now, let's read verses 14-20."

> *Afterward he appeared to the eleven themselves as they were reclining at [the] table, and he rebuked them for their unbelief and hardness of heart, because they had not believed those who saw him after he had risen. And he said to them, "Go into all the world and proclaim the gospel to the whole creation. Whoever believes and is baptized will be saved, but whoever does not believe will be condemned. And these signs will accompany those who believe: in my name they will cast out demons; they will speak in new tongues; they will pick up serpents with their hands; and if they drink any deadly poison, it will not hurt them; they will lay their hands on the sick, and they will recover." So then the Lord Jesus, after he had spoken to them, was taken up into heaven and sat down at the right hand of God. And they went out and preached everywhere, while the Lord worked with them and confirmed the message by accompanying signs.*

"Jesus gathered the eleven apostles together to give them a gigantic task. You would remember that Judas had betrayed Christ and later killed himself, right?" When Katie and I nodded, Devin continued. "He told the eleven to preach the gospel to the entire world! There was, of course, a hefty obstacle in their way of doing so. They were fishermen, not linguists. How were they to convince the whole world that Jesus Christ had risen from the grave?" Devin read verse 20 again.

And they went out and preached everywhere, while the Lord worked with them and confirmed the message by accompanying signs.

"God gave them the ability to perform miracles in order to convince the world. Tell me, you two; how do you know that Jesus came to earth to die and be raised for the whole world?"

"The Bible says so," I said confidently as Katie nodded in agreement.

"Right. And the apostle John even tells us in John 20:30-31 that the reason why he recorded Jesus' life and miracles was so that we would have the ability to read and believe. However, there was a time in history when the Bible was not completely written, but people still needed to believe it."

Devin was right, but I had never thought about that before. I tried to put myself in the first century. How would I react if a dozen men came up to me, claiming that their friend had risen from the grave? I would not have believed it even if a hundred people claimed it.

"In history, whenever God sent a messenger to deliver a new message, he gave his messenger the ability to perform miracles in order to confirm the message. Moses had the signs of the staff, leprosy, and blood. Elijah raised a boy from the dead. Jesus healed the blind. Because of these miracles, the audience believed the message, even though they didn't have 'book-chapter-verse.' Does that make sense to you?"

"Yeah, it does," Katie said thoughtfully.

"Good. Well, one of the miracles that Jesus gave to the apostles was the ability to speak in tongues." Devin then turned his Bible to another passage. "We'll look at this other passage in context, too. The end of Acts 1 tells us that Matthias was added to the eleven apostles to take Judas' place. Then chapter 2 begins. This is, perhaps, the best chapter we have to understand the gift of tongues. Remember that it was these uneducated fishermen's job to teach the whole world the gospel." He then read verses 1-4.

> *When the day of Pentecost arrived, they were all together in one place. And suddenly there came from heaven a sound like a mighty rushing wind, and it filled the entire house where they were sitting. And divided tongues as of fire appeared to them and rested on each one of them. And they were all filled with the Holy Spirit and began to speak in other tongues as the Spirit gave them utterance.*

"This happened in Jerusalem on the day of Pentecost, which was a Jewish feast that Jews from all around the world attended. Verses 5 through 11 tell us what it means to speak in tongues."

> *Now there were dwelling in Jerusalem Jews, devout men from every nation under heaven. And at this sound the multitude came together, and they were bewildered, because each one was hearing them speak in his own language. And they were amazed and astonished, saying, "Are not all these who are speaking Galileans? And how is it that we hear, each of us in his own native*

language? Parthians and Medes and Elamites and residents of Mesopotamia, Judea and Cappadocia, Pontus and Asia, Phrygia and Pamphylia, Egypt and the parts of Libya belonging to Cyrene, and visitors from Rome, both Jews and proselytes, Cretans and Arabians— we hear them telling in our own tongues the mighty works of God."

Devin stopped reading to let us react. I was thankful, since I really needed to think about what I just heard. It seemed that Devin was showing me something from the Bible that again went against what others had taught me. Had they used the Bible? No, but Devin had. If only I had read all of this chapter, I would have learned it on my own. Perhaps, 'Pastor John' needed to read it, too.

Devin handed me the Bible. "What was their question in verse 4?"

"How was it that these people from different countries heard these uneducated men speaking in their own languages?"

Devin took the Bible back from me and handed it to Katie.

"What was their observation in verse 11?"

"The mighty works of God were being told in their own tongues."

"Based on what the Bible says, what does it mean to speak in various tongues?" Devin asked the both of us.

Handing the Bible back to Devin, Katie answered, "To speak in different languages."

"When people in the Bible spoke in tongues, did their audience understand the words coming out of the tongue-speaker's mouth?"

"Yeah, they really did," I said. I was astonished.

Katie and I waited for Devin to continue. He seemed to be collecting his thoughts. Finally, he began, "I don't know about your experiences, and I don't want to diminish your sincerity, but from what I see in the religious world today, many who claim to speak in tongues do so by uttering unintelligible speech. Something is going on that they'll never be able to naturally explain. However, whatever they're doing, it's not biblical tongues."

Katie and I looked at each other, but we didn't say anything. I wonder if she was thinking the same thing I was. *How many times is this going to happen?* Once again, Devin had shown to me a simple Bible truth by simply turning to and reading a passage. How much deception had I swallowed? How many others in my life were in the exact same position? Every time I had heard someone "speak in tongues," it was unintelligible speech. A stranger likely would have called it babble. Now that I thought about it, it didn't make a lot of sense, anyway, having God give a person the ability to speak gibberish in order to prove he or she was saved.

Shifting in his seat, Devin broke my deep thought. "This passage in Acts 2 is the first passage in the Bible where someone had the miraculous gift of tongues. It makes sense, too, since Christ just gave the apostles the commandment to preach the gospel to all nations. Imagine being an uneducated fisherman with the burden of that commandment on your shoulders!"

"I could hardly imagine!" Katie broke in.

Raising a finger, Devin continued, "But God, in his power and wisdom, gave the apostles an opportunity to do just that in a matter of days after the commandment."

"You're talking about the big Jewish festival, right?"

"Yes. People from all around the world were gathered. Supreme opportunity. With his new ability to speak in languages he had never studied, verse 14 tells us that Peter, standing with the eleven other apostles, started teaching the people about the wonderful news of Christ. That's an amazing mixture of both providence and miracle!"

"What's the difference?" I asked.

"Providence is where God uses forces already in play to make something happen or not happen. Making sure that the apostles were ready and gathered to preach at the same time and place as this crowd that was ready and gathered to hear—that was God's providence. A miracle, however, is when God breaks the rules of nature to make something happen. Healing a paralyzed man on the spot, turning water into wine, and being able to speak in an intelligible language without previously studying it—those are all examples of miracles. God has worked through providence from the beginning until now. Miracles, however, happened a bit differently. Let's keep studying about the miracle of tongues, shall we?"

I leaned back in my chair and gave a sigh. It wasn't that I was completely surprised at the evening's revelation. I was still a bit upset from having been deceived. I was also very concerned about the sincerity of all of my friends. How was it that they were convinced to the core that what they were doing was an example of biblical tongues? Like Devin said, they would never be able to explain it. However, they also could not defend it with the Bible. I sat up straight in my chair. "That's what we're here for, right?"

"Yes." Devin refocused his eyes on the Bible. "I want you to try to imagine what a first century worship assembly would have been like." He turned to First Corinthians 13. "Imagine living back then and hearing about an assembly of this new group called 'Christians.' You're curious, so you go to visit them. Today, when we want to preach an authoritative message, it's easy for us to teach that Jesus said in John 8:24 that if you don't believe in him, you will die in your sins. However, it was a bit harder for the first century Christians to preach the same message, since the book of John, being written by the apostle about sixty years after Christ's resurrection, was one of the last books of the Bible written. Instead of pointing to book-chapter-verse, certain Christians of the first century were given the gifts of prophesy and miraculous knowledge until the Bible was completed."

"I had never thought about that!" I said with wide eyes. "So, there was a time when the world needed to believe everything about Jesus, yet the New Testament wasn't available. That must have been hard for those preachers to convince people."

"Without God's help, it certainly would have been. But we must remember Mark 16:20." Holding a finger in First Corinthians 13, Devin quickly turned to Mark 16."

And they went out and preached everywhere, while the Lord worked with them and confirmed the message by accompanying signs.

"That's how they overcame the obstacle, huh?" I continued as Devin nodded. "Of course, I would believe someone's message if he was able to work the miracles mentioned in that passage. It's coming together for me."

"I'm seeing it, too," Katie chimed in.

Devin flipped back to where his finger was in his Bible. "Another obstacle that was in the way of all this preaching was, once non-Jewish people were added to the church, there were potentially several different languages represented in any given assembly. That's where the gift of tongues came in. Would you mind reading verses 8-13 of First Corinthians 13, Lance?"

Love never ends. As for prophecies, they will pass away; as for tongues, they will cease; as for knowledge, it will pass away. For we know in part and we prophesy in part, but when the perfect comes, the partial will pass away. When I was a child, I spoke like a child, I thought like a child, I reasoned like a child. When I became a man, I gave up childish ways. For now we see in a mirror dimly, but then face to face. Now I know in part; then I shall know fully, even as I have been fully known.

"God never intended for miraculous gifts to be permanent in the church. He allowed for miraculous gifts in order to produce faith in the gospel's audience until it could be perfectly written down through the inspiration of the Holy Spirit. As John finished his gospel account," Devin turned to John 20:30-31, "he said:"

Now Jesus did many other signs in the presence of the disciples, which are not written in this book; but these are written so that you may believe that Jesus is the Christ, the Son of God, and that by believing you may have life in his name.

"John knew that we would have to depend on an accurate record in order to fully believe in Christ. Thank God for the accurate record!" Devin held his Bible up in the air. "That's why Paul could say in Romans 10:17, 'So faith comes from hearing, and hearing through the word of Christ.'"

"And you're saying that once the Bible was completed, all the miracles in the church went away, even tongues?" I asked.

"It doesn't matter what I say," Devin pointed to himself. "But I'd be happy to explore this Scripture with you. Look back at First Corinthians 13 with me. In verses 8 and 10, we see that love never ends, but the gifts of prophecies, tongues, and miraculous knowledge would end when that which is perfect would arrive, since those gifts, according to verse 9, are partial. Verse 12 says that we can know fully once that perfect thing comes"

"I could see how that would be the Bible," Katie said.

"Before the Scriptures were completed, people had good reasons to be skeptical of a resurrected Lord. That was until they saw the wonders of the preachers' hands. However, how many miracles do we have to see today to believe in this risen Lord?" Devin raised his Bible in the air again.

"Absolutely none," I said with resolve. "Sure, I have doubted things, but the Bible stands up against all scrutiny, doesn't it?"

Devin nodded. "Yes, but that's a different study for a different time."

"I believe," I said. "And it's all because of what I have read in that amazing book. Devin, you're helping me so much, and I have to thank you again, even though I sense we're not finished here."

Katie broke in. "What about those people who are working miracles today, even on TV? I see what you're saying and all, but how do you explain all of that if miraculous gifts aren't being given today?"

"That's a good question. Like I said earlier, I don't want to take away from anyone's sincerity; however, we read last night that sometimes we can be sincere, but sincerely wrong. 'There is a way that seems right to a man, but its end is the way to death,'" Devin said, quoting Proverbs 14:12. "In Mark 16, along with healing, Jesus mentions the gift of tongues and immunity to poison. In the book of Acts, we see the apostles raised the dead and healed the lame, not just 'back problems,' but paralysis! Who is doing those things on TV today?"

"No one," Katie said, shaking her head.

Devin turned to Matthew 7:21-23. "This passage tells us that many people are going to be surprised on the day of judgment. Included in that group is a bunch of people who think they're going to heaven because they 'performed many miracles.' Look here."

> Not everyone who says to me, "Lord, Lord," will enter the kingdom of heaven, but the one who does the will of my Father who is in heaven. On that day many will say to me, "Lord, Lord, did we not prophesy in your name, and cast out demons in your name, and do many mighty works in your name?" And then will I declare to them, "I never knew you; depart from me, you workers of lawlessness."

"That's a scary passage!" I said.

"Lance, if I recall correctly, the whole reason why you wanted to study this is because your friends told you that you needed to speak in tongues in order to know you're saved, right?"

"That's right. In fact, they told Katie the same thing."

Katie nodded in agreement.

"First," Devin continued, "the Bible does tell you that you can know you have eternal life." Devin turned to First

John 5:13. He pointed and said, "Read that verse for us."

I write these things to you who believe in the name of the Son of God that you may know that you have eternal life.

"As we saw earlier, at the end of his gospel account, John tells us that he wrote so that we would believe. Then he tells us that he writes this document so that we may know we have eternal life. You see, the Bible never says you are given the gift of tongues for that purpose. The Bible simply asks the question, 'Have you done what is written?' If so, you can know you have eternal life, because God keeps his promises."

I picked up the notes I made on the passages Pastor John gave me. "What about this, though?" I pointed to the second passage, Acts 2:38. "Does this not happen anymore?"

"You mean God giving the gift of the Holy Spirit to those who repent and are baptized?"

"Yeah. Is that gone, since the Bible is complete?"

"Absolutely not. Read it again, and then read the next verse." Devin quickly found the passage and handed the Bible to me.

And Peter said to them, "Repent and be baptized every one of you in the name of Jesus Christ for the forgiveness of your sins, and you will receive the gift of the Holy Spirit. For the promise is for you and for your children and for all who are far off, everyone whom the Lord our God calls to himself."

Devin followed up, "Passages like First Timothy 2:4 tell us that God wants all to be saved, and according to Second Thessalonians 2:14, God calls people to himself through the gospel. God wants to fulfill Acts 2:38 for every single person. Now, read Acts 5:32."

I found the passage quickly, since I was already in the book of Acts.

> *And we are witnesses to these things, and so is the Holy Spirit, whom God has given to those who obey him.*

"So, God gives his Spirit to the obedient," Devin said, "and I know for sure that this isn't the same gift as being able to speak in tongues by the power of the Spirit, since at the end of Acts 10, a group of people speak in tongues before they get baptized in water. The question is, how does the Spirit work in these people's lives? The Bible has the answer."

"Devin, I'm not surprised to hear you say that, and I won't be surprised if you know where to find it," I said smiling and shaking my head.

"I might have something to show you," Devin said, returning the smile while finding Ephesians 1:13-14.

> *In him you also, when you heard the word of truth, the gospel of your salvation, and believed in him, were sealed with the promised Holy Spirit, who is the guarantee of our inheritance until we acquire possession of it, to the praise of his glory.*

"You see, when God saves someone from the grips of Satan, he seals that soul with his Holy Spirit. That person is still in this world, being subject to temptation and death; however, he or she has heaven to look forward to, which will be the absence of those things. It's kind of like putting earnest money on a house. You don't fully possess it yet, but no one else is allowed to buy it or even make an offer, since you've invested in it."

"That's a powerful illustration," I said.

Katie had picked up and started fidgeting with the pen from the notebook. I could tell she was thinking deeply on the things we had discussed throughout the evening. I was right there with her. How my thinking had been changed!

"Not only that, but the Spirit also helps Christians with communication with God." He turned to and started reading Romans 8:26.

> *Likewise the Spirit helps us in our weakness. For we do not know what to pray for as we ought, but the Spirit himself intercedes for us with groanings too deep for words.*

"When a Christian's heart goes up to God, but the words aren't working right, according to verse 27, the Spirit intercedes for the saints."

"That's very comforting," Katie said.

"There's no wonder why the Spirit is called the Comforter in John 16." Devin gave a warm smile.

"Wait, you said the Spirit helps the saints?" I asked. "Aren't those dead people?"

Devin choked back a chuckle. "Yes, some saints have died, but I know what you're referencing. Many religious people think you can only become a saint after you die on earth. That's hardly the truth. The Bible uses *Christians*, *disciples*, *the church*, and *saints* interchangeably, meaning that they all refer to the same group of people."

While Devin spoke, Katie got up, rearranged some chairs in the room to form a makeshift couch, and lay down on the formation.

That can't be comfortable, I thought, allowing a smile to

emerge. It was getting late, and I was just as tired as she was—maybe more so, since I had worked a full shift that evening.

"A saint is simply someone who has been set apart for God. For instance, when Paul greets the church in Corinth in First Corinthians 1:2, he greets *the church*, and then he calls them *saints*. Peter, in Acts 9:32, took his ministry to the *saints* who were *living* in a town called Lydda."

"So, the whole 'voting on a dead saint thing' is all made up?" Katie asked.

"Unfortunately, it's just another example of someone rejecting the word of God in order to follow the trad—"

"—traditions of men," I finished with palpable disappointment. *God, how tragic the deception of the religious world is!* I silently prayed. *I wonder why you let it get so bad.* I couldn't sit still any longer, so I stood up to pace. There was a war going on inside of me, several battles having already been fought. Everything I had been taught and held on to so tightly seemed to be challenged by the teachings of Scripture. Of course, the Bible had won every battle. How many more would there be?

"You okay?" Devin questioned.

"Yeah, it's just frustrating. I've been deceived by those who have been deceived."

"I know exactly what you mean," Devin said, standing. "Deception is Satan's best tool. In the Garden, Adam and Eve were not convinced to become Satanists. Instead, the Devil made them think they were becoming more like God! In Second Timothy 3, right before Paul told Timothy how powerful Scripture is, he prophesied that evil people would not only deceive, but they would become deceived themselves. Satan doesn't have to get us to turn our backs completely on God. All he has to do is convince us that any lie is true."

"I've certainly believed a lot of religious lies in my lifetime."

"You're not alone, man. Me too. So far, the times we've spent looking at the Bible together, it's been on topics you've brought up. There are two topics I'd really like to show you in the Bible. Based on Katie's posture, I don't think we're ready for much more tonight."

"What? It's comfortable!" Katie defended herself with a giggle.

Still smiling, Devin turned to me, "When's your next day off?"

"Thursday."

"I've got Thursday off, too. How about you and Katie come over to my apartment for some pizza, and we explore the Scriptures some more?"

"Sure! Sounds good to me," I confirmed.

"I don't know," Katie said. "I'll have to get back to you. I'll let Lance know."

"Alright. Do you guys have your own Bibles?"

We both confirmed that we did.

"Bring them with you. There's always something special about reading the truth out of your own copy."

Death Sentence

Thursday, July 31, 2003; Henderson, Tennessee

Having grown up in the town, finding Devin's house was no problem. He was living in a duplex on one of the back streets of Henderson. With my leather-cased maroon Bible in hand, I approached the door.

"Katie couldn't make it?" Devin asked as he opened the door.

"No," I said, allowing my smile to neutralize. "She said she doesn't want to study anymore."

"Really? What's up?"

"She didn't say exactly. She seemed pretty positive the other night. I was sure she learned just as much as I did."

"That might be the problem," Devin said, showing me a chair at the table. "The pizza should be here in fifteen. I just ordered it."

"What problem? What do you mean?"

"Let me show you. Find Mark 10 with me."

For the first time, I opened the leather case with real purpose. I was convinced that I was about to learn more from this maroon Bible in one session than I had learned from it in the five years I had owned it. I looked over at Devin's Bible to find the whereabouts of Mark.

"Mark is the second book of the New Testament. Matthew, *Mark*, Luke, and John."

After we both found Mark 10, Devin had me read verses 21 and 22.

> *And Jesus, looking at him, loved him, and said to him, "You lack one thing: go, sell all that you have and give to the poor, and you will have treasure in heaven; and come, follow me." Disheartened by the saying, he went away sorrowful, for he had great possessions.*

"This rich, young ruler wanted eternal life, as you can see in verse 17," Devin pointed in my Bible. "But when he learned how much it was going to cost him, he turned away from the opportunity to be with Jesus. Many people still do this today, and maybe that's what Katie has done. When people encounter a challenging teaching of Scripture, they turn away from it, because it's easier just to 'go with the flow' than to actually convert to the truth. Do you know what I mean?"

"Absolutely," I said with a nod. "More so than I ever thought possible. I've been convinced for a decade that I had faith that would get me to heaven. The past few days, however, have taught me that I was riding the faith of others, and it was a false faith at that! My 'faith,'" I inserted air quotes, "has never required anything of me. Now, I'm having to completely refocus and make it my own faith. On one hand, I'm enjoying the things you're teaching me, but on the other hand, I'm agonizing over it."

"Why?" Devin asked. He didn't really say the word with a question in his voice. Instead, he said it the way a counselor might say it. He wanted me to put it out on the table and wrestle with it. That's exactly what I needed.

"I keep asking myself, 'Where is this leading?' and, 'What does it imply if I accept what the Bible teaches?'"

As a good counselor, Devin then asked, "And what conclusions are you coming to?"

"Where is it leading? Well, it could lead to one of two things, heaven or hell, right?"

Devin didn't say anything.

"I suppose I could do what everyone else is doing. I could just do what I've always done. I could pretend I'm alright with God, accept any and all religious teachings, but I don't think that will lead me to heaven. What does it imply if I accept the teachings of the Bible? I'll tell you exactly what it means. It means that my parents are wrong, but they're sincerely wrong. Their hearts are good; they just haven't pursued the truth far enough, just like so many other people." I started thinking of people who have had an impact on my spiritual life in my past. Mom, Dad, Grandma, Grandpa, Derek, Mrs. Laura, Keith the youth pastor, Mick, Bob, Pastor John. I loved all of these people in one way or another, and none of them had purposefully misled me.

Devin broke my silent concentration. "Are you going to follow in the Mark 10 man's footsteps? In Katie's footsteps?"

I looked up and met Devin's eyes. "No. Eternity is a long time. Whatever it costs me on earth is nothing compared to eternity."

"You're right. Satan is using every means possible to make every person possible as comfortable as possible on this temporary world. He doesn't want us thinking about eternity. As long as you keep eternity in your mind and heaven as your goal, you'll make it there." Devin then had us both turn to and read Matthew 10:34-39.

Do not think that I have come to bring peace to the earth. I have not come to bring peace, but a sword. For I have come to set a man against his father, and a daughter against her mother, and a daughter-in-law against her mother-in-law. And a person's enemies will be those of his own household. Whoever loves father or mother more than me is not worthy of me, and whoever loves son or daughter more than me is not worthy of me. And whoever does not take his cross and follow me is not worthy of me. Whoever finds his life will lose it, and whoever loses his life for my sake will find it.

"It was true in the first century just the same as it is today," Devin continued. "Choosing to follow Christ means rejecting everything else, even your own life. No, you won't have to literally take your own life or disown your parents. However, you must be willing to sacrifice anything that could get in between you and heaven. It's important that you face this fact now, before you get much deeper. In Luke 14, Jesus compares discipleship to building a tower or fighting a battle. You must count your money before beginning a building project, right?"

"It's foolish not to," I agreed.

"Similarly, before someone challenges an opponent on the battlefield, he does so only after he has confirmed his army is mightier than his enemy's. Do you have enough to beat Satan?"

"I'll do everything I can," I said with resolve.

"Let me show you the danger of losing the battle. Second Peter 2:20-22."

For if, after they have escaped the defilements of the world through the knowledge of our Lord and Savior Jesus Christ, they are again entangled in them and overcome, the last state has become worse for them than the first. For it would have been better for them never to have known the way of righteousness than after knowing it to turn back from the holy commandment delivered to them. What the true proverb says has happened to them: "The dog returns to its own vomit, and the sow, after washing herself, returns to wallow in the mire."

"Peter warns us here," Devin said, pointing to the passage, "that if we make the commitment to follow Christ, but then turn away from that commitment later on, it will be worse for us than before we even made the commitment, like taking a shower and then swimming in mud, or vomiting up poison and then slurping it back up!"

"That's gross, dude!" I said, scrunching up my face.

"It makes an impact, doesn't it? Let's try to remember the analogies Peter makes any time we're tempted by Satan."

"Wait a minute," I interjected. "You're saying that once we're saved, we can lose our salvation? When I was saved several years ago, my youth pastor told me that now that I was saved, I would always be saved."

"We're not God's puppets. We're his children. We always have a choice. It is true that Christ will never turn his back on us; however, the Scriptures have plenty of passages that warn Christians about the temptations and consequences of falling back into sin. For instance, consider Hebrews 10:26-27."

For if we go on sinning deliberately after receiving the knowledge of the truth, there no longer remains a sacrifice for sins, but a fearful expectation of judgment, and a fury of fire that will consume the adversaries.

"The context assures us that the author is writing to Christians, and he tells them how to lose access to the blood of Christ. Just go on sinning willfully!"

That, of course, made sense. I didn't remember much else that the youth pastor taught. However, that "once saved, always saved" teaching stuck with me, because I interpreted it as a license to sin. How immature that was!

The doorbell rang. "Cowabunga! Right on time!" Devin said, getting up.

"Right on time for what?" I asked.

"Anytime pizza's at the door, it's on time!"

Over dinner, Devin and I continued to chat about the commitment to Christ, and what it really meant to be a disciple. "It's the most important decision anyone can make," Devin pointed out. "It's more important than where you go to college, who you marry, and what you name your kids. *This* decision," he emphasized, "will determine everything else—every decision you make on earth and where you spend eternity."

Pizza boxes empty and hands purified from grease, we retrieved our Bibles. Opening his, Devin said, "The main passage I wanted to show you this evening is in Romans 6. Let's begin with verses 16 through 18."

> *Do you not know that if you present yourselves to anyone as obedient slaves, you are slaves of the one whom you obey, either of sin, which leads to death, or of obedience, which leads to righteousness? But thanks be to God, that you who were once slaves of sin have become obedient from the heart to the standard of teaching to which you were committed, and, having been*

set free from sin, have become slaves of righteousness.

"Jesus said in Matthew 6, 'No one can serve two masters.' This passage mentions two masters, sin and righteousness." Devin held out his hands as if he was holding the two options. "*Righteousness* means to be right with God. If we choose to sin, we choose to be slaves to sin. However, if we choose obedience, we choose to be slaves to righteousness; we dedicate our lives to being right with God. Look again at verse 17. These people used to be slaves to sin, but what did they do in order to change that?"

"It says they became obedient."

Devin waited for me to finish. When I didn't say anymore, he asked, "That's not all it says, right?"

I looked closer at the text. "From the heart."

"And that's key," Devin said, raising a finger. "Sure, we can make a list of commandments and check them off, but God's not interested in mindless, emotionless obedience. If he was, he would have created computers, not humans. There are two options. Either you are a slave to sin or you're obedient from the heart, becoming a slave to righteousness, completely dedicated to being right with God. There's no neutrality."

"What do you mean that there's no neutrality?"

"Most religious people these days depend on something that's not there. I like to call it the lie of the middle ground. Many people are standing on ground that doesn't exist. A lot of people picture Jesus on the judgment day with scales that measure good works versus bad works. Meaning they expect Christ to put the good things they have done in life on one side, and the bad things on the other side. As long as they didn't kill, rape, or steal on a regular basis, they're good to go. That's not how it works. Look at John 12:48 with me."

The one who rejects me and does not receive my words has a judge; the word that I have spoken will judge him on the last day.

"It won't be your good works versus your bad works; it will be your life versus God's word! Will you measure up?" Devin asked.

"What do you mean? Are you asking if I have done what the Bible says?"

Devin slowly nodded.

"Definitely not always."

"So, you're saying you've sinned?"

"Absolutely."

"Do you know what Romans 6:23 says?"

"No idea."

"The wages of sin is death." Devin let that sink in. "You see," Devin began in a slower tone, "God's justice demands punishment for sin."

"Yeah, I learned that concept a few weeks ago," I said, remembering my impromptu conversation with Bob during a break from band practice.

"Good. I'm glad you understand it. A couple of days ago, I showed you First John 5:13, which tells us we can know we have eternal life if we have done what is written."

"I remember that. That was during the study on tongues."

"Yeah. So, you've admitted to me that you haven't done what is written. You've sinned. What does that mean for you?"

"Well, not only can I not know I am saved, but from what you're telling me, I can't be saved! Is that right?"

"You're jumping to conclusions on that last part. I didn't say you can't be saved. I'm saying that you're just like me. Since I've sinned, too, you and I don't *deserve* to be saved. I quoted to you Romans 6:23 a moment ago, but I didn't do so in its entirety. I wanted you to understand what the first bit really meant before we read the rest. God's justice demands punishment for sin, and it's been that way since the beginning. That's where grace comes in. Will you read Romans 6:23 for us?" Since we had turned away from Romans 6, it took me a moment to find it again. Devin was patient.

> For the wages of sin is death, but the free gift of God is eternal life in Christ Jesus our Lord.

There it is again, I thought. *The justice and love of God in one verse.* Just three weeks prior, Bob and I had spent some time discussing what it meant for God to be both *just* and *all-loving*. God is absolutely pure; therefore, sin goes against his perfect nature. He, as the judge of the world, honestly has to deal out punishment for sin. At the same time, however, he loves everyone, and he does not want us to face the punishment, so he sent his Son to die in our stead.

> God shows his love for us in that while we were still sinners, Christ died for us. Romans 5:8.

I had been one of those living the "lie of the middle ground," as Devin had put it. I had always thought I was living a *generally* good life. Yes, I had dabbled in things that were obviously sinful, but I had never really hurt anyone in the process. How wrong I was! I had hurt myself desperately in the process, severing my relationship with God. He had created me, intending me to be his child, and I had completely rejected his love by giving Christ hundreds—thousands—of reasons to die for me alone. *Forget the "bad" people. I alone killed Jesus.* I thought I was "good enough" to get to heaven, but the Bible was slowly teaching me that there is no "good enough." You were either completely sinless, which was out of the question for me; you were under God's grace, completely dedicated to the Lord; or you were a sinner on the road to destruction.

> *Enter by the narrow gate. For the gate is wide and the way is easy that leads to destruction, and those who enter by it are many. For the gate is narrow and the way is hard that leads to life, and those who find it are few.* Matthew 7:13-14.

Only two roads, I reminded myself. Jesus said it was *easy* to be on the road to destruction. How true that was for me. How long had I lived by the phrase, "go with the flow"? Too long. *I'm either right with God, or I'm not. I'm either on my way to heaven, or I'm on my way to hell. Which one?* Was I living for God? I made the resolve right then and there to make the changes in my life required for me to be able to say *yes* to that question.

We still had our Bibles open to Romans 6. "Verse 23, along with other passages, tells us that salvation is a gift." Devin leaned over to point to the word *gift* in my Bible. "But, just like any gift, we have the choice to accept it or reject it, but as Hebrews 2:3 suggests, we will not escape the wrath of God if we neglect the salvation that God offers us. We must accept it on his terms. As we saw in verse 17, we've got to become slaves to righteousness, completely dedicated to our Lord. We've got to become obedient from the heart."

"What about faith?" I asked. I didn't ask it as an excuse,

since I imagined many people probably played the faith card as an excuse to live however they wanted to live, just as I had. "Where does faith come into all of this obedience?"

"Please don't misunderstand me. You're absolutely right that faith is important and cannot be missed. In fact, Hebrews 11:6 tells us that 'without faith it is impossible to please him, for whoever would draw near to God must believe that he exists and that he rewards those who seek him.' We need to start treating Jesus as the great physician he is, according to Matthew 9, instead of some fairytale. The world has this idea that having faith in Jesus is simply acknowledging his existence, just like believing in Santa Claus. Jesus isn't a jolly man in a red suit. He is the great physician, who calls sinners to repentance. How often do you go to the doctor?"

"Maybe once in the past ten years," I said with a chuckle.

"Stubborn guy. I understand. Well, imagine you had a doctor you had to visit frequently. If he proved himself to be a good doctor, you would start having faith in him, wouldn't you?"

"Yeah, I suppose so. Go on."

"Picture yourself going into his office with your stomach in absolute knots. You're desperate to be healed, and you ask him, 'Doc, what do I need to do?' Then he tells you. What do you do?"

"I'd do what he says. No brainer."

"Why is that?"

"I suppose it goes back to the faith thing, doesn't it?" I started to understand Devin's point.

"Yep. Turn to Hebrews 5." Devin read verses 8 and 9.

Although he was a son, he learned obedience through what he suffered. And being made perfect, he [Jesus] became the source of eternal salvation to all who obey him

"This passage says that Jesus provides eternal life to those who obey him. But John 3:16 says that those who believe will have eternal life. So, which one is it?"

"It's gotta be both."

"Exactly. It's not either-or. It's both. That's why James 2:26 warns us that faith without works is dead. Next, let's look at First John 3:4. Will you read that one for us?"

Everyone who makes a practice of sinning also practices lawlessness; sin is lawlessness.

"Obedience is so key to our relationship with God that disobedience, or *lawlessness*, as John puts it, is sin. This includes disobeying both the don'ts and dos. You have convinced me today of how serious you are about making sure you're right with God."

"I'm willing to do whatever it takes!" I pictured Christ going to the cross on my behalf. I certainly owed him my loyalty. *Loyalty* wasn't the right word. I wasn't his pet. I was supposed to be his child. I owed him my life and more!

"Good. Then it's time for you to die."

"Excuse me?" I didn't know what Devin was getting at. Certainly he wasn't literally threatening my life... right?

"You've got to die, and you have to do it as soon as possible. You'll understand what I mean when you read the first 2 verses of Romans 6."

That was a relief. Mentioning a passage like that meant he

was using figurative speech... right? Again, I didn't know how sure I was of that. I turned to the passage and read reluctantly.

> *What shall we say then? Are we to continue in sin that grace may abound? By no means! How can we who died to sin still live in it?*

"See? You have to die. You've got to die to sin."

It was figurative. However, it wasn't much easier than it would have been if the Bible had been using literal speech. Again, Devin was teaching me what I desperately needed, but what I did not want. I had lived for years doing as I pleased. I had been pleased with "surface faith" and the "lie of the middle ground." Of course, I finally understood that neither of those would get me to heaven. Being absolutely comfortable with hypocritical Christianity, my faith had never required anything of me. I never had to get out of my comfort zone. I never felt compelled to stand up for the truth. I never had to say *no* to something for the sake of faith. I never had to say *yes* to something for the sake of faith, either. I had been doing the impossible: serving two masters.

> *No one can serve two masters, for either he will hate the one and love the other, or he will be devoted to the one and despise the other. You cannot serve God and money.* Matthew 6:24.

Though I was not necessarily pursuing literal money, I was definitely materialistic, and I was on my personal throne.

> *For what does it profit a man to gain the whole world and forfeit his life? For what can a man give in return for his life?* Mark 8:36-37.

The words went through my head again. *Die to sin.* After

some time, I met Devin's eyes. "There are some changes I have to make in my life. You don't have to tell me. I need to start living for Christ. I need to start really living for him. For too long I have fooled myself and my friends." In a matter of a few minutes, I had moved from being comfortable to disgusted with my hypocritical lifestyle.

"I think you're starting to understand repentance. When you're ready, I want us to look at one more passage tonight, Second Corinthians 7:10."

"I'm ready," I said, already looking for the passage.

> *For godly grief produces a repentance that leads to salvation without regret, whereas worldly grief produces death.*

"I know you're starting to feel bad," Devin said in a soft tone. "Bad for your sins. Bad for the life you've been living. I'm not going to pat you on the back and say, 'There, there. It's okay,' because it's not okay. It's not okay that you and I both have messed up a lot. We've given Jesus a reason to die. If you're anything like me, we've both given him thousands of reasons to die. Let that produce in you what this passage talks about: godly grief, because that will produce repentance."

"I thought grief was repentance."

"That's a common misunderstanding. Feeling sorry and saying you're sorry are part of it, but it's got to be proven. Repentance is complete when it produces real change. Repentance is a mind, heart, and body thing—a change of mind, a deep grief, and a change of action." Quoting Matthew 3:8, Devin said, "We don't just say we're sorry, but we 'Bear fruit in keeping with repentance.' We all have a throne in our lives. Priority number one is always on that throne. Most people decide to put themselves there.

Jesus says, however, 'Deny yourself, take up your cross, and follow me.' Who's on your throne?"

"I'm putting Christ there right now. Living for myself has only driven me further and further from heaven."

"That's the most rewarding, yet the most difficult decision to make. I'm so glad you've made that decision, my friend. But there's still one more thing we must study about. Are you working tomorrow?"

"Yeah."

"Me, too. Are you doing anything after work?"

"Not yet."

"Can we spend some time after work looking at one more subject?"

"Sure. What is it?"

Devin grabbed a paper towel from the roll on the table and wrote, "The Gospel—First Corinthians 15:1-4." He handed it to me and said, "The book of Second Thessalonians says that those who do not obey the gospel," he pointed to the paper towel, "will suffer eternal destruction. That's what I want to study about—obeying the gospel."

"Where does this passage come in?" I pointed at the towel.

"Take this home, and find out. Tomorrow, I want you to tell me the three main points of the gospel."

"More homework, huh? Fair enough. I look forward to it." My Bible was still open to Second Corinthians 7, so, before zipping it up, I quickly found First Corinthians 15 and closed the paper towel in the Bible as a bookmark.

Though the study was over, I stayed at Devin's house for

the rest of the evening. We played some video games. We discussed movies. We listened to techno music with booming bass. We ate greasy potato chips. We became closer friends.

When I finally got home, before going to bed, I unzipped my Bible to do my homework. Finding my bookmark, I read First Corinthians 15:1-4, looking for "the gospel."

> *Now I would remind you, brothers, of the gospel I preached to you, which you received, in which you stand, and by which you are being saved, if you hold fast to the word I preached to you—unless you believed in vain. For I delivered to you as of first importance what I also received: that Christ died for our sins in accordance with the Scriptures, that he was buried, that he was raised on the third day in accordance with the Scriptures*

I recognized the passage right away. It was the same passage the sermon was on when I went and visited the church where Lydia attended. That day, the preacher, too, put a lot of emphasis on the gospel. In verse 1, Paul said he was presenting the gospel. Then he explained how the gospel affected their lives. Then he plainly said that the gospel was the death, burial, and resurrection of Jesus Christ. *That wasn't so hard*, I thought. Devin really was helping me in many ways, whether or not he knew it. I was finally able to look at Scripture systematically, instead of "skipping and dipping."

Streetlight Conviction

Friday, August 1, 2003; Henderson, Tennessee

Devin and I clocked in at 4:30 pm the next day. He was on grill, and I was on chicken. Going back to the kitchen together to wash our hands and get ready, I whispered, "I did my homework."

"Great. Did you find the gospel?" Devin responded in a low voice.

"Yep. The death, burial, and resurrection of Jesus."

"Good job, my friend!"

"Actually," I started to admit, "I had help. That's the passage that Lydia's pastor preached on last Sunday when I visited the church."

"I'm glad you've spent some time studying," Devin said, "that gives us a head start for tonight. Let me caution you, though. The guy who preached for you last Sunday was likely not one of Lydia's pastors. In the Bible, those who preach the gospel are not pastors. They're called evangelists, which means they are people who preach the good news, the gospel, since *gospel* means *good news*. The word *pastor* is found in only one verse in the Bible, Ephesians 4:11, and it tells us that pastors and evangelists are two different workers in the church. So, the guy who preached on Sunday was likely an evangelist, not a pastor."

"Wow. That must be another one of those traditions of men, huh?" In the Lutheran, Baptist, and Apostolic churches, we always called the preacher the pastor. I was once again reminded of how much of my life I had not spent studying or understanding God's word. How much was I going to ask God to sacrifice for me before I was willing to sacrifice something for him?

"Hey, it's a common misconception. You're right, though. It's a tradition of men." Changing subjects, Devin surprised me by asking, "Are you saved?"

"Of course I am."

"Man, that is excellent. Remember how I told you last night that Second Thessalonians says that those who do not obey the gospel will suffer eternally?"

"Yeah. That was pretty heavy stuff."

"Tonight, if you get some time to think while working with your chickens, be thinking of your salvation experience. I want you to walk me through it later. Try to remember how and when you were saved. Also, I want you to try to tell me whether or not you have obeyed the gospel. Is that alright?"

"Sure. These chickens never have much to say, anyway, so I'll have plenty of time to think."

Devin smiled. "Good. Once again, though, we're putting our jobs on the line. We'd better zip it until after work."

"Agreed."

In the two and a half years I worked at the restaurant, I handled over 20,000 chickens. In my mind, I had become a professional chicken cleaner and cooker. The chicken duty was the least desired job, yet I was scheduled for it more than anyone else, because of my proficiency. I didn't mind so much. Being good at my job gave me plenty of time to think.

Between clock in and clock out that evening, I spent time thinking about my salvation. The first time I believed I got saved was at the youth rally Derek and I went to. I had prayed for Jesus to enter my heart and forgive me. At the end of that night, I felt great. The youth pastor told us that Jesus saved us that night, and Derek and I were convinced we were headed to heaven. That was almost six years prior to when I met Devin.

However, just recently, I had allowed 'Pastor John' to dunk me in water. Why? Because I wanted to know that I was saved. Since I had not spoken in tongues like he and the people of the Apostolic Church, I was told that there was no way for me to know I was saved. Devin, using the Bible, was able to show me that their teachings regarding salvation and tongues were not right.

I am saved, right? I started going through the past month's events, putting special thought on the studies I had gone through with Devin. *Nothing this past month has convinced me of my salvation.* If anything, it had convinced me that I hardly knew anything about the Bible. That was, of course, until Devin showed a special interest in my soul. Devin had shown me that we can know we have eternal life by comparing our lives to what has been written. *Have I done what has been written? What about the gospel? Have I obeyed it?*

Coming in from his break later that evening, Devin said to me, "It's a nice night out there tonight. How about we spend some time out there after work?"

"You mean have the study outside?"

"Yeah, under the lights of the parking lot."

"Sounds like a nice plan."

Later, after all customers were gone, all dishes were cleaned, all equipment was stowed, all floors were mopped, and all doors were locked, Devin and I both went to our respective vehicles. We didn't do so in order to drive them, but to retrieve our Bibles from them. Sitting on the curb of the parking lot, we began.

"Have you thought much about my questions tonight?" Devin started.

"Quite a bit, actually."

"I hope you don't mind sharing. We've spent a lot of our time together with me pointing and sharing. Now, it's your turn. Would you mind sharing some of your experiences with me?"

"No, I don't mind." I told him about the youth rally and the Sinner's Prayer. He knew about my recent baptism, but I expanded on that, too.

"Just so I understand it the best I can," Devin began with a thoughtful look, "you were saved when you went to that youth rally and invited Jesus into your heart? You were saved through that prayer?"

"As far as I know, yes. This past month has made me question a lot of things I had previously understood, though."

"Other than your baptism a couple of weeks ago, were you ever baptized before that?"

"Yeah. I guess I should have told you. You know I grew up as a Lutheran, so my family had me baptized when I was a baby."

"Was it by sprinkling, pouring, or immersion?"

"They sprinkle for baptism in the Lutheran Church," I said. I assumed that I was baptized the same way.

"In all of your life, have you ever obeyed the gospel?"

"That question is what occupied my mind the most tonight. You agreed that the gospel is the death, burial, and resurrection of Jesus, right?"

"Simply, yes." Devin continued, "But, since the word *gospel* means *good news*, then the good news involves Jesus in his entirety. But in First Corinthians 15, Paul says that the death, burial, and resurrection is of 'first importance.' It is the pinnacle, the high point of the good news."

"That's what I thought. How is it that I can obey an event? I thought we obeyed commandments. I don't see a commandment in that passage."

"I see your confusion. Hopefully, it'll be cleared up soon enough. Thank you for sharing some of your past with me," Devin said with a somber voice. "I know all of this is special for you. You find people at their sincerest moments when they either go through or recount religious experiences. It sets the stage for a great study we're going to have tonight. Before we begin, do you have any questions or anything else you'd like to share?"

"No. I suppose that's about it."

"Well, then it seems you'll be interested in starting with obeying the gospel. Let's read Second Thessalonians 1:7-9." While we flipped to find the passage in our Bibles, Devin said, "In context, Paul is trying to encourage Christians who were suffering persecution. He's telling them that they have a reward waiting, whereas those who mistreat the church will suffer God's wrath. Would you mind reading for us?"

> *and to grant relief to you who are afflicted as well as to us, when the Lord Jesus is revealed from heaven with his mighty angels in flaming fire, inflicting vengeance on those who do not know God and on those who do not obey the gospel of our Lord Jesus. They will suffer the punishment of eternal destruction, away from the presence of the Lord and from the glory of his might.*

"According to verse 7, who will Jesus punish on that day?"

"Those who do not know God and those who do not obey the gospel," I said with some familiarity on the last bit.

"That's right. I just needed you to see it for yourself in your own Bible. We're going to switch gears for a moment and focus on some blessings that Jesus Christ offers us. Turn to Romans 6:23. We looked at that passage last night."

> *For the wages of sin is death, but the free gift of God is eternal life in Christ Jesus our Lord.*

"The blessing in Christ is eternal life, right?"

"Yeah. I see that."

Devin then showed me Colossians 1:13-14 and Second Timothy 2:10, which say that forgiveness of sins and salvation are also found in Christ. "Not only that, but Ephesians 1:3 tells us that every spiritual blessing is in Christ. Therefore, how many blessings are outside of Christ?"

"Logically, none," I said.

"Not only is it logical. It's also biblical. Now, turn to Galatians 3:26-27."

for in Christ Jesus you are all sons of God, through faith. For as many of you as were baptized into Christ have put on Christ.

"How did these people prove their faith?"

"They got baptized."

"What did baptism do for them?"

Without a doubt, I could see it right there. "It placed them into Christ!"

"And how many spiritual blessings, including salvation and eternal life, are found in Christ?"

"Every single one," I said.

"Can someone partake of these spiritual blessings if they have not obeyed God in the act of baptism?"

"Apparently not."

"Let's be turning to Acts 2. We've already read verse 38 before, but now that we're looking at what the New Testament teaches about baptism, we should read it again."

And Peter said to them, "Repent and be baptized every one of you in the name of Jesus Christ for the forgiveness of your sins, and you will receive the gift of the Holy Spirit."

"If these people wanted the forgiveness of sins, what were they to do?"

"Repent and be baptized."

"Correct. Before someone can be biblically baptized, they have to die to sin first. You told me that you were sprinkled with water as a baby?"

"Yes."

"And they called that baptism?"

"Yeah. I even have a baptismal certificate."

Devin smiled. "I suppose that's important, since it's impossible for a baby to remember what happens when he's only a month or so old." Then Devin got a pen out of his pocket and offered it to me. "Would you like a bite of my candy bar?"

"What?"

"Yeah, I know it doesn't look like chocolate, but it's sweet!"

"What are you getting at, man?"

Devin held up his blue-capped pen in the light shining above us. "How many times do we have to call this a candy bar before it becomes one?"

"Not gonna happen."

"But what if we got church leaders calling it a candy bar for a thousand years?"

"Not gonna happen."

"That's my point exactly. Like I said earlier, I know your experiences are important to you, but forgive me when I tell you the truth. When someone sprinkled water on your forehead, there's no way that was biblical baptism. They might have called it baptism. Clergy in the Catholic Church and other churches have called that baptism for years. You even have a certificate! But you cannot confirm it with God. Let me show you what I mean." Devin then instructed me to turn and read Acts 8:36-39.

> *And as they were going along the road they came to some water, and the eunuch said, "See, here is water! What prevents me from being baptized?" And he commanded the chariot to stop, and they both went*

down into the water, Philip and the eunuch, and he baptized him. And when they came up out of the water, the Spirit of the Lord carried Philip away, and the eunuch saw him no more, and went on his way rejoicing.

Devin pointed to verses 27 and 28. He said, "This eunuch was traveling from Jerusalem to Ethiopia. That trip would have taken weeks. Surely, he would have had some water with him. But, in order for Philip to baptize him, they had to find some water, go down into it and come up out of it."

"So, that's why the Apostolic Church dunked me completely under water!"

"Most likely, yes. Look at Colossians 2:12 as well."

having been buried with him in baptism, in which you were also raised with him through faith in the powerful working of God, who raised him from the dead.

"Paul said these people had been buried in baptism. They were also raised. If you were to bury someone, do you sprinkle or pour just a bit of dirt on them?"

"No. You completely cover them."

"That's why biblical baptism must be a burial in water. Every time baptism is described in the Bible, it uses words like 'go down,' 'much water,' 'come up,' and 'burial.' If I start sprinkling people and call it baptism, does sprinkling become baptism?"

"Not for a second. Just like your pen will never be a candy bar!" We both laughed when Devin started biting on his pen with a sour face.

"That brings us back to our passage in Acts 2. Peter said they had to repent of their sins before they were baptized. The passages we studied last night showed us that repentance involves deep sorrow and a change of action.

How many babies have the capacity to do that?"

"None that I know of."

"That's why no babies in the Bible were ever baptized. Let's go back to our favorite chapter. Romans 6. Remind me again of the three points of the gospel."

"The death, burial, and resurrection of Jesus," I said without hesitation.

"You asked me earlier how someone could obey that, since it's a historical event. I think you'll see the answer in this passage. Look at verses 1-4."

> *What shall we say then? Are we to continue in sin that grace may abound? By no means! How can we who died to sin still live in it? Do you not know that all of us who have been baptized into Christ Jesus were baptized into his death? We were buried therefore with him by baptism into death, in order that, just as Christ was raised from the dead by the glory of the Father, we too might walk in newness of life.*

Devin and I had spent so much time in the chapter already, but I had never seen these verses before. I would not have been so confused about 'obeying the gospel' if I had just simply read the rest of the context of all the verses Devin and I had read together in this chapter. It wasn't a long chapter, either. I could have just exerted a bit of effort to learn so much. Oh, how much truth I had missed out from God's word because I was lazy or afraid! How many people have been in the same position that I was in? Religious leaders have convinced us that only the "clergy" is able to understand the Bible. Right then and there, in the restaurant parking lot, nothing could have been further from the truth. I was not trained in theology. I disdained my literature classes at school. I didn't read for pleasure. Yet there I was, understanding the words of the most important book in history without problem.

The gospel comprised of the *death, burial,* and *resurrection.* All who want to avoid hell must obey the gospel by *dying to sin,* being *buried in baptism,* and *raising to walk a new life.* He or she will then be *in Christ,* and Second Corinthians 5:17 claims, "if anyone is in Christ, he is a new creation." I had realized in my life that some questions felt "heavier" than others. There was a question that came to my mind in that parking lot that was "heavier" than any question I had ever pondered before. *How many people are headed to hell right now because they haven't taken the time to simply read the Bible?*

> *But Jesus answered them, "You are wrong, because you know neither the Scriptures nor the power of God."* Matthew 22:29.

Devin was silent. He could tell something was sinking in. It was sinking in deeply.

I met his eyes. "I understand now. To obey the gospel, you've got to repent and be baptized, so you can be raised to a new life."

"There's no wonder why Jesus calls it being 'born again' in John 3," Devin said, nodding at my understanding. "Let me show you one more piece of the salvation puzzle. Do you remember what the Bible says about the church? We studied it that first night in the shed."

"Yeah. There is only one church of Christ."

"What was another word for the church?"

"Sorry. I can't remember."

"It's alright. Ephesians 1:22-23 tell us that the church is the *body* of Christ."

"That's right. I remember now."

"Good. Well, Ephesians 5:23 tells us that Jesus is the Savior of the body. Do you remember that?"

I nodded, readying my fingers to turn to a new passage.

"Turn to First Corinthians 12:12-13."

> *For just as the body is one and has many members, and all the members of the body, though many, are one body, so it is with Christ. For in one Spirit we were all baptized into one body—Jews or Greeks, slaves or free—and all were made to drink of one Spirit.*

"This passage tells us that, though there is only one body of Christ, each member of the church is an important member of his body. If we read through the rest of the chapter, we'd see just how important the members of Christ's church are. However, I wanted you to see what verse 13 says."

"I already see it," I said. "We join the church by being baptized into it."

"That's partially correct. First, we become part of the church when we're biblically baptized. You're right about that. However, the Bible never says anyone joins the church. Instead, over and over, the Bible says the Lord adds people to the church when they obey the gospel. For instance, as we read the commandment to repent and be baptized in Acts 2, if we continued reading, we would see 3,000 people were baptized, and the Lord added them to the church as they were being saved."

"Ok. That makes sense. I guess going around and joining the church of your choice would be another tradition of men."

"Unfortunately, it's a very popular tradition. Speaking of

traditions, I need to bring up another one of your past experiences. You told me that when you were in the sixth grade, you were saved when you said the Sinner's Prayer, right?"

"Yeah. At the youth rally."

"Have you ever seen the Sinner's Prayer in the Bible?"

"I guess I haven't read the Bible enough to find it."

"Me either. By the way, no matter how much we read the Bible, even from cover to cover, we will keep saying the same thing—'I still haven't found it!' And that's because it's not there."

"Prayer isn't in the Bible?"

"That's not what I mean. Of course, prayer is in the Bible. But never do you see someone getting saved by," Devin made some air quotes, "'inviting Jesus into their heart and praying for forgiveness.'"

"Whoa, really?"

"Really. The Sinner's Prayer is a hoax. It was invented by a man, and it wasn't even very popular until a famous man started preaching it in the last century."

I was knocked back. Almost every time I heard a sermon at the Baptist Church, it ended with an invitation to say the Sinner's Prayer—to become a Christian, to become saved, by "inviting Jesus into your heart." "Surely the people who preach the prayer thing have some Bible verse they use!" I said.

"You're right. Unfortunately, they do," quoting Second Peter 3:16, he continued, 'which the ignorant and unstable twist to their own destruction, as they do the other Scriptures.' The two main passages they use as proof-texts are Romans 10:9 and Revelation 3:20. Their folly is in their lack of effort. If they would only understand the context, they would quickly learn that these passages were written to Christians, people who were already saved. It all goes back to our important question. Who is speaking to whom?"

"It's easier to say a prayer than to obey the Bible in baptism," I said. *How many people have been deceived? Millions upon millions. Satan doesn't have to work hard to keep people out of heaven. All he has do is make the wide road easy, and convince the people on it that they are headed in the right direction.*

> *Enter by the narrow gate. For the gate is wide and the way is easy that leads to destruction, and those who enter by it are many. For the gate is narrow and the way is hard that leads to life, and those who find it are few.* Matthew 7:13-14.

Devin interrupted my heartbreak over the deception in the world. "They say you can be saved by saying a prayer." He had turned his Bible to Mark 16:16. Handing it to me and pointing to the verse, he asked, "But what does Jesus say about salvation?"

> *Whoever believes and is baptized will be saved, but whoever does not believe will be condemned.*

"There's effort on our part," he said. "We've got to read it. We've got to believe it. We've got to obey it." Quoting Second Thessalonians 1:8, he said, "'in flaming fire, inflicting vengeance on those who do not know God and on those who do not obey the gospel of our Lord Jesus.' Lance, have you obeyed the gospel?"

My first reaction was to say, "Absolutely!" I had felt saved in the past. Yet I had also been deceived by my feelings before. I had recently been baptized, but that was a very confusing decision. I hardly even knew what I was doing. I was just interested in following another deception, which was modern-day "tongue-speaking." Finally, I answered, "I don't know."

"Well, that's an answer you're going to have to figure out. Let's go through some things. What has to happen before someone is baptized?"

"They've got to believe.," I said, referring to Mark 16:16.

"Yes. Plus, they have to repent of their sins, Acts 2:38. What does that mean concerning your infant baptism?"

"Since I was in no state to be doing either of those as an infant, it didn't mean anything to God, not to mention the fact that I was sprinkled and not buried."

Devin pursed his lips and nodded his head in response. "What about your 'Sinner's Prayer'?"

"It's an invention by men, though millions have believed it, it has never saved anyone, not even me." The weight on my shoulder was getting heavier. In normal circumstances, I would have responded by jumping up and shouting, "Who are you to judge me?" But I knew that every single one of these observations came straight out of the Bible. If I were to accuse anyone of judging that night, it would have had to been God. Who was God to judge me? He was my Creator. He wanted to be my Father. What was I going to do to make his wish a reality? I grappled for anything to hold on to. I turned to Devin, "But I felt great that night, after saying that prayer."

"That's the craftiness of Satan. Proverbs 14:12 says, 'There is a way that seems right to a man, but its end is the way to death.'"

"Yeah, I remember you quoting that one before. You're right. I thought I was on the right path, but I had believed a lie."

He pushed the conversation forward. "A couple of weeks ago, you were dunked under water. Why did you do that? What was it for?"

"My friends told me that I would be able to speak in tongues after I was baptized. That's what I did it for. Again, I had believed Satan's deception." I didn't blame my friends, since they were in the same boat I was in.

"Can we read Acts 2:38 again?" he asked. I agreed to do so.

> And Peter said to them, "Repent and be baptized every one of you in the name of Jesus Christ for the forgiveness of your sins, and you will receive the gift of the Holy Spirit."

"What should someone really get baptized for?"

"For the forgiveness of their sins."

"Let's read Ephesians 4:4-6."

> There is one body and one Spirit—just as you were called to the one hope that belongs to your call—one Lord, one faith, one baptism, one God and Father of all, who is over all and through all and in all.

"Just like there is one Lord and one body, how many baptisms does God approve of?"

"Just one." It was as clear as clear could be.

"In Acts 19," Devin continued, "the apostle Paul went to Ephesus, and he found a group of people claiming to be disciples, so he started asking them about their baptism. Let's read verses 3-5."

And he said, "Into what then were you baptized?" They said, "Into John's baptism." And Paul said, "John baptized with the baptism of repentance, telling the people to believe in the one who was to come after him, that is, Jesus." On hearing this, they were baptized in the name of the Lord Jesus.

"Had these people been baptized before?"

"Yes."

"Was it the one baptism that is commanded today, the baptism for the forgiveness of their sins?"

"Apparently not."

"And what did they do when they realized it?" Devin asked.

"They did the right thing. They were baptized for the right reason."

"Notice," Devin began with a soft tone, "that Paul did not question their sincerity. He didn't berate them. He didn't condemn them. He simply made sure they had an opportunity to make things right with the Lord. Lance, I'll ask you again. Have you obeyed the gospel?"

I knew the answer this time. Sure, I had been 'baptized,' but I was calling a pen a candy bar. Neither one of my 'baptisms' was the one baptism in the Bible. "No. I haven't."

"You understand that obeying the gospel requires a death, burial, and resurrection, right?"

"Yes. More than ever."

"What will you do regarding sin in your life?"

Again, if it were anyone else other than Devin, this man

whom I had gotten to know and gained so much respect for in a matter of months, I would have turned that question back on him. I would have avoided all sin in my life and pointed out the hypocrisy in his life. Devin had told me more than once, though, that he had been in this same situation not too long ago. He was floating along, trying to live a "good enough life," not depending on the righteousness of God, being completely comfortable in half-hearted denominationalism. To answer his question, I said one word. "Repent." My heart was breaking. I had given Christ so many reasons to die on my behalf.

"No longer to live in it?"

"I'll do my very best."

"That's what the Lord asks of you. Since you're dying to sin, what do we need to do with that dead body?"

I looked back at Devin with resolve. "It needs to be buried."

"In Acts 22:16, a man named Ananias asked a man named Saul a very important question. Let's pretend it's the Lord asking you this question, okay?"

"Sure."

God's providence had been working my entire life to get me to that very moment. Why had my mother decided to move to Henderson, Tennessee, although she had no friends or family in the entire southern region of the United States? Why had I gotten the job at the restaurant without even an interview? Why had I recently met musicians who were spiritually minded, giving me the same mindset? Why had the band ended right as the seeds of the gospel were being planted into my heart? The answer was clear. God's wisdom. He was leading me to that very moment. Devin read the verse to me.

And now why do you wait? Rise and be baptized and wash away your sins, calling on his name.

I am a dead man walking, I thought to myself later that night. I had gone home. Devin had impressed upon me how important the decision was to get baptized. The truth was clear to me. Yes, I had religiously gotten wet before, but I had never been biblically baptized. I had made the decision to turn away from the lifestyle of sin. Continuing with the biblical analogy, I needed to bury that old man of sin in the water grave of baptism.

Before I left the parking lot, I had asked Devin some more questions about sin. "Does repentance mean that you'll never sin again?"

"Oh, no," Devin responded. "If we say that we do not sin, the truth is not in us." Devin directed me to First John 1:5-10, which, as Devin had said, gave him hope over almost any other passage.

But if we walk in the light, as he is in the light, we have fellowship with one another, and the blood of Jesus his Son cleanses us from all sin. 1 John 1:7.

"After rising to walk a new life, we will have constant access to the blood of Christ, which will continue to work wonders in our lives," Devin said. "That's why we're baptized into his death, as Romans 6 indicates."

Devin had informed me in the parking lot that water was not hard to come by, and I could be united with Christ in his death, burial, and resurrection in a matter of minutes. The weight of the truth was still heavy on my shoulders. Many petty thoughts came to mind. Temptation to completely flee the truth flitted here and there, too. In the end, I told Devin that I would meet him in the morning, and we would do it then. Satan was working hard.

It was late when I got home. The house was dark, though my mother had left the back porch light on, as she always did for me. Years of navigating the kitchen and hallway allowed me to get to my bedroom silently, without turning on any lights. Even when I got to my room, I opted for darkness and silence, although my habit was to quickly turn on some music. My room was in the opposite wing of the house as my mother and step-father's.

I removed the grease-infested uniform and sat on my bed to think. I was a dead man sitting. *I'm ready for my newness of life*, I thought. I began to pray to God to help me, as I knew being a completely converted person to Christ was not going to be easy. I had spent so long in the world of sin. Plus, beside Devin and Lydia, all of my friends were very worldly. All of them were materialistic, most of them used filthy language, many of them were social drinkers (more like social *drunkards*), some of them did drugs, and even a few were thieves. Having dabbled in some of their deeds of darkness with them, most would not understand the next times I refused to participate. *How will I be treated at school?* The new school year, my senior year, was just a matter of days away.

> *By faith Moses, when he was grown up, refused to be called the son of Pharaoh's daughter, choosing rather to be mistreated with the people of God than to enjoy the fleeting pleasures of sin.* Hebrews 11:24-25.

I was ready to say *no* to the pleasures of sin and say *yes* to the one who died for me. Before thinking any further on how my "friends" and classmates would treat me, I snapped out of it. I knew the longer Satan could get me to focus on such thoughts, the more he had me in his grasp. I needed to take my thoughts away from Satan once and for all and make them captive to the obedience of Christ, just as Second Corinthians 10:5 taught.

Devin assured me that my new family in Christ would rally around me, always being ready to lift me up and encourage me. "It just shows another aspect of God's wisdom. Christianity is a *family* thing, not an *individual* thing. We'll pray for you and with you. We'll be with you every step of the way."

Reborn

Saturday, August 2, 2003; Finger, Tennessee

The next day, I was thankful to be able to avoid the questions that would have inevitably come from my mother if she saw me leaving the house again with a change of clothes and a towel. My mother had left the house early to go shopping with my aunt, as was customary for the two of them on at least one Saturday of each month.

At about 8:30 am, I got into my Blazer and followed Devin's directions to the building where the church of Christ met in Finger, Tennessee, which was about fifteen minutes from my home. Devin's white van was already there, being the only vehicle in the parking lot. Devin was standing outside of it with an elderly man wearing overalls. When I approached, the man extended his hand.

In a soft voice, he said, "My name's Kurt. I'm one of the deacons of the church. You've made the best decision of your life, son. I'm glad to be here to witness it."

"He lives nearby, and he's going to let us in," Devin said. "Are you ready to be united with Christ?"

I was somber but decisive. "Without a doubt," I said in a steady voice. "Lead the way, Mr. Kurt."

Kurt unlocked the front double-doors and led us into a modest foyer. Beyond the entrance, there were rows of wooden, padded pews, surrounded by wooden walls, and covered by a wooden ceiling. The small building could have held about 175 people comfortably. There was a lectern on a small platform at the back of the building, facing the doors we had just entered. Kurt went behind the lectern and pulled a curtain string, revealing a permanent baptistery already filled with water.

"Is it always full?"

"They don't close down the hospitals, do they? You never know when someone's going to decide to be born again. It's always full. It's always ready," Kurt said in his gentle voice.

He then showed us a room to the side of the baptistery. Not only did the church always keep the baptistery full and ready at all times, they also kept a stash of towels in the side room. Though I didn't need one of their towels, I was happy to have the private room for changing out of wet clothes after the baptism.

There was a set of steps and a door in the room, which led to the water. Kurt unlatched the small door and allowed Devin to get in first. Devin rolled up his sleeves and began to go down into the water.

A moment later, I stood at the top of the steps and looked down at the man who had become such a dear friend to me in a matter of months, the man who would later be the best man at my wedding. Never had I met a person like Devin. I was so thankful to have met him, since he was the first person to properly introduce me to Jesus Christ. I took my first step of four down into the baptistery. I didn't bother adjusting any of my clothes, since I intended to get completely wet. *I need to be absolutely sure to bury this old man of sin all the way,* I silently told myself. *I want a new person to come out of that grave.* Having completely descended into the water, the water line reached my chest.

Devin smiled at me. "It's a special day, Lance."

"Yes it is," I responded.

Devin then had me stand where it would be easiest for him. He gave me advice on how to prevent the water from going up my nose. Though those instructions were helpful in preventing discomfort, I knew they were overall inconsequential, so long as I was buried in the water. After all, the entire reason why I had to obey Christ in baptism was because of the discomfort I had personally caused him. *Discomfort? What an understatement!* Every sin I had ever committed had given Christ another reason to suffer the torment he received on this earth—the disbelief of others, the mocking, the shame, the pain, the separation from his Father.

And Pilate again said to them, "Then what shall I do with the man you call the King of the Jews?" And they cried out again, "Crucify him." And Pilate said to them, "Why, what evil has he done?" But they shouted all the more, "Crucify him." So Pilate, wishing to satisfy the crowd, released for them Barabbas, and having scourged Jesus, he delivered him to be crucified. Mark 15:12-15.

And the people stood by, watching, but the rulers scoffed at him, saying, "He saved others; let him save himself, if he is the Christ of God, his Chosen One!" The soldiers also mocked him, coming up and offering him sour wine and saying, "If you are the King of the Jews, save yourself!" Luke 23:35-37.

Now from the sixth hour there was darkness over all the land until the ninth hour. And about the ninth hour

Jesus cried out with a loud voice, saying, "Eli, Eli, lema sabachthani?" that is, "My God, my God, why have you forsaken me?" Matthew 27:45-46.

After this, Jesus, knowing that all was now finished, said (to fulfill the Scripture), "I thirst." A jar full of sour wine stood there, so they put a sponge full of the sour wine on a hyssop branch and held it to his mouth. When Jesus had received the sour wine, he said, "It is finished," and he bowed his head and gave up his spirit. John 19:28-30.

"Lance," Devin began, "Have you repented of your sins, having made the decision to follow Christ for the rest of your life?"

"Yes, I have," I responded loud enough for Kurt to hear, who was sitting and smiling on the front pew.

"Do you believe that Jesus Christ is the Son of God and that he died on the cross to save you from the punishment of your sins?"

"Yes. More than ever."

"Excellent." Devin was smiling from ear to ear. "Based on your confession, I now baptize you in the name of the Father, Son, and the Holy Spirit, for the forgiveness of your sins."

I plugged my nose with both hands. Devin's large, right hand grabbed both of my wrists at once, while his left hand supported my back. With the force of his right hand, he plunged me into the grave, where I contacted the blood of Christ.

Devin had told me the night before that baptism is like surgery. It removes the sin from a person's life the way a doctor removes skin from a baby when he is circumcised.

"That's a funny analogy," I had said.

"To us, yes, but to the Jews of the first century, it was completely relevant."

> *In him also you were circumcised with a circumcision made without hands, by putting off the body of the flesh, by the circumcision of Christ, having been buried with him in baptism, in which you were also raised with him through faith in the powerful working of God, who raised him from the dead. And you, who were dead in your trespasses and the uncircumcision of your flesh, God made alive together with him, having forgiven us all our trespasses, by canceling the record of debt that stood against us with its legal demands. This he set aside, nailing it to the cross.* Colossians 2:11-14.

For the two seconds I remained under the water, I could almost feel the surgical scalpels of Christ. In some areas of my life, he needed chisels. I was completely immersed, completely wet; however, I was not taking a physical bath, but a spiritual one.

> *Baptism, which corresponds to this* [Noah and his family on the ark], *now saves you, not as a removal of dirt from the body but as an appeal to God for a good conscience, through the resurrection of Jesus Christ.* 1 Peter 3:21.

I had been living a life completely captivated by sin. Though the world would not have necessarily called me a "bad person," I was just as guilty of rejecting my Savior as the ones who physically drove the nails into Christ's body. I had been separated from God for so long, as Isaiah 59:1-2 taught. In that moment, fulfilling his wonderful promise in Scripture, God was uniting me with the death of and burial of Christ.

> *Do you not know that all of us who have been baptized into Christ Jesus were baptized into his death? We were*

buried therefore with him by baptism into death, in order that, just as Christ was raised from the dead by the glory of the Father, we too might walk in newness of life. For if we have been united with him in a death like his, we shall certainly be united with him in a resurrection like his. Romans 6:3-5.

Having completely submerged my body under the water, I felt Devin reverse directions. His left hand pushed up, while his right hand eased the pressure. My face broke a smile while my body broke the surface of the water. It was then that I was raised to walk a new life. My sins were washed away. I was surprised to see that the water was still clear, not blackened by my lifelong commitment to sin. However, it was not the water that was working. It was God's commitment to his promise.

Whoever believes and is baptized will be saved. Mark 16:16a.

I was finally a true Christian. In that very moment, the Lord had added me to his church. Back on my feet as a new creation in Christ, my first reaction was to hug my mentor. Any hopes in keeping the top portion of his shirt dry dissolved under my waterlogged hug.

"Congratulations, my brother," He said. "Welcome to Christ."

"Thank you so much, Devin. Thank you for leading me to him."

Devin put a hand on each of my shoulders. He met my eyes and said, "You are now a Christian according to the pattern of the New Testament. Be a Christian for the rest of today. Be a Christian for the rest of your life. Do so, and receive the promise found at the end of Revelation 2:10."

I didn't bother asking Devin what that verse said. I knew it was something splendid. Memorizing his Scripture reference, I thanked him again.

After we separately toweled off and changed into dry clothes, we met Kurt back in the auditorium. Devin asked the gentle old man to lead a prayer over us, and he did so simply, yet eloquently.

Devin was scheduled to work that day, so he and I departed separately, discussing our plans to meet at the same place for worship the following day.

My mother was still gone with my aunt when I got home. My step-father was working, so the house was empty. Against my customs, I again opted for silence. I picked up the leather case to find Revelation 2:10, looking for a promise. I found it.

> *Be faithful unto death, and I will give you the crown of life.*

Transformed

August 2003 - Present Day (August 2013)

The first months, and even years, of pure, New Testament Christianity proved God, Devin, and me right. God was right about having fellowship with other believers and access to his Son's blood (1 John 1:5-10). Devin was right about the church being a family (Acts 2:41-47). I was right about the difficulty of staying out of the world (Hebrews 12:1-3). I was a changed person inside. My Spirit was willing, but my flesh was weak (Matthew 26:41).

> *For those who live according to the flesh set their minds on the things of the flesh, but those who live according to the Spirit set their minds on the things of the Spirit. To set the mind on the flesh is death, but to set the mind on the Spirit is life and peace.* Romans 8:5-6.

There were times when I slept in by choice on Sunday, instead of participating in the blessing of fellowshipping with the saints in the worship of the Lord. I was a foolish time-waster.

> *Look carefully then how you walk, not as unwise but as wise, making the best use of the time, because the days are evil. Therefore do not be foolish, but understand what the will of the Lord is.* Ephesians 5:15-17.

I had been baptized into Christ, and the promise is, "if anyone is in Christ, he is a new creation" (2 Corinthians 5:17). It didn't take me long to realize why the Bible calls it "newness of life" and being "born again" (Romans 6:4; John 3:3-5). Stumbling and falling are frequent for babies learning to walk. But, eventually, they get the hang of staying vertical. Then they have to work on walking straight. It's a progression, and good parents are there every step of the way, just like our heavenly Father is there to help us as we learn. Being born again certainly was not the end of my journey. It was the beginning of a new life in Christ.

Though I was immature, I did my best to change day by day, and I did so by the grace of God. I tried to represent Christ in all that I did. Sometimes, I succeeded. Sometimes, I failed, either by misquoting Scripture or doing something completely contrary to what I knew God wanted for my life.

God surely is a forgiving God. He showered his grace on me day by day. He kept me going when I lost friends to the world.

> *The time that is past suffices for doing what the Gentiles want to do, living in sensuality, passions, drunkenness, orgies, drinking parties, and lawless idolatry. With respect to this they are surprised when you do not join them in the same flood of debauchery, and they malign you; but they will give account to him who is ready to judge the living and the dead.* 1 Peter 4:3-5.

The above passage came to life before my eyes just weeks after I became a Christian, when my final year of high school began. Over the summer, my entire life had changed. However, my friends did not. They thought it strange when I turned down their drinking, piracy, and drug usage. They thought it strange that I didn't join them for their "senior year celebrations." Once school started, and I was once again surrounded by my peers, it was difficult to not dive right back into my old ways. God, however, reminded me through Scripture and other Christians that fellowship in the body of Christ is the closest thing to heaven on earth there is. After some time, fellowship with the body of Christ trumped rebellious partying any day.

In January 2004, I went on a trip to the mountains with a local church's youth group. I knew many of the youth group from high school, so it was easy for me to graft in. The trip was designed for the youth to enjoy spiritual growth and further develop their relationships with each other, and so it did. During the second night of the trip, however, the three guys I was rooming with (fifteen, sixteen, and seventeen years old) came in late. It took about five seconds for me to realize they had snuck out to go boozing. These guys had been raised in Christian homes their whole lives. Since childhood, they had been exposed to the truth that I had recently learned about— the truth about Christ that I left everything to pursue. I couldn't believe they were so easily trampling the Son of God underfoot. That night, I preached my first sermon, and my entire audience responded with repentance.

Again, the kingdom of heaven is like a merchant in search of fine pearls, who, on finding one pearl of great value, went and sold all that he had and bought it. Matthew 13:45-46.

In December 2004, my biggest faith-shaking experience hit me. I had started classes at the Selmer, Tennessee, campus of the University of Tennessee Martin. Many of my classes met in the evening. On my way home from class on Thursday evening, I answered a phone call from my mother. With a very heavy voice, she delivered to me the news that one of my closest friends, my brother-in-law, had been killed in a car accident.

His funeral was the first I had ever participated in. His funeral was the first I had attended. Questions flooded my life. I already knew some of the answers. Some more answers came from Scripture. Some of the questions, however, remained unanswered.

During this time in my life, I saw the rallying power of the church. Prayers were lifted up publicly on my behalf, even in an assembly of nearly 400 people. I received cards from strangers. Expressions of sympathy and love flowed from my brothers and sisters in Christ. One day, an acquaintance at church quietly hugged me. She then handed me a tract, which was titled, "Death Hurts. But Jesus Helps." As the tract prompted, I read John 11, which proved the title of the tract true.

It must have taken the Romans a while to grasp this "newness of life" concept. In the same letter in which Paul had to remind them of their baptism and new lives in Christ, he had to beg them to complete the transformation process.

> *I appeal to you therefore, brothers, by the mercies of God, to present your bodies as a living sacrifice, holy and acceptable to God, which is your spiritual worship. Do not be conformed to this world, but be transformed by the renewal of your mind, that by testing you may discern what is the will of God, what is good and acceptable and perfect.* Romans 12:1-2.

Day by day, I grew in Christ.

> *But by the grace of God I am what I am, and his grace toward me was not in vain.* 1 Corinthians 15:10a.

Not long into my Christian walk, I heard about some opportunities for full-time evangelistic work. I had learned of the support system that God established in the church. Missionaries in the New Testament were financially supported by the body of Christ in different cities, so they could go to other cities and spread the gospel. *How wonderful that would be if I could do that!* The day I heard about such work, a seed was planted deep into my heart. It would take years to be watered and finally bloom, but it was a seed that changed all my future plans.

After my first year at UTM, I decided to transfer to Freed-Hardeman University to continue my degree in Fine Arts. I knew that UTM was a party school, and it would be no good for my faith. FHU had many Christians on its campus that would help me grow to new heights.

It was in Drawing class at FHU where I met the beautiful woman who would later become my wife. Throughout our courtship, Kristen challenged me to be a better man of God, always encouraging me to live by faith in Jesus Christ.

One day during the summer after our wedding and a month after I graduated with my bachelor of Fine Arts, I came home from work ignited. The afore mentioned missionary seed had sprouted without warning. I was not satisfied with the idea of secular work for the rest of my life. Sure, I could have worked hard at a graphic design firm, making a comfortable sum of money, but for what? To leave it all behind? I wanted to change lives.

I spent the evening explaining to Kristen my thoughts, and we made the decision together to dedicate the rest of our lives to spreading the gospel. We had never conducted a Bible study before, but we had both been on the receiving end of many. We knew the power was in the word, and not in us.

We had made the decision to become missionaries of the gospel of Christ, although we had no idea what to do next. That did not remain an obstacle, since God opened door after door after door for us. Our elders at the Finger, Tennessee, church sent us to the nation of Bonaire and the state of Vermont to help located missionaries spread the gospel. Though we were sent to "help," the workers on the field helped us by showing us the mission field first-hand. I also received a job preaching the gospel in Finger, which served as my training ground before Kristen and I left for the mission field, though we understood that everywhere, even our neighborhood, served as a mission field. While working and living in Finger, Kristen and I learned what it was like to have the full-time job of spreading the soul-saving gospel. Our elders did their God-given jobs extremely well, shepherding us the whole way.

Now, Kristen and I reside in Porirua, New Zealand, fulfilling the Lord's great commission, which started with eleven men.

> *And Jesus came and said to them, "All authority in heaven and on earth has been given to me. Go therefore and make disciples of all nations, baptizing them in the name of the Father and of the Son and of the Holy Spirit, teaching them to observe all that I have commanded you. And behold, I am with you always, to the end of the age." Matthew 28:18-20.*

Jesus' eleven apostles (later twelve and thirteen) taught thousands. Those thousands taught thousands more, who taught the next generation. Centuries later, Christ's influence reached my family. My parents were the first to teach me the story of Jesus Christ. I am the better for it, and I am eternally grateful for their willingness to teach me about the man on the cross. In due course, the gospel transformed the life of a Texan, who eventually moved to Henderson, Tennessee, in order to attend school. As a fast food burger-flipper, Devin had the choice to talk about the world or talk about Christ. In the summer of 2003, he stepped out in faith and mentioned the most important person in his life to a new acquaintance. Devin "explained to [me] the way of God more accurately" (Acts 18:26). Devin will never know how much I appreciate his willingness to do so.

> *I have been crucified with Christ. It is no longer I who live, but Christ who lives in me. And the life I now live in the flesh I live by faith in the Son of God, who loved me and gave himself for me.* Galatians 2:20.

This Has Been for You

The words you have read in this project labeled *Conformed, Reborn, Transformed* have been written for *you*. I wanted to share my journey of faith with you in hopes that you would discover the truth that has set me free. Are you willing to be bold enough to "abide" in the word of Christ? After all, his word is what will judge you in the end—not your conscience, not your religious leaders, not your family—but the word of Christ.

> So Jesus said to the Jews who had believed in him, "If you abide in my word, you are truly my disciples, and you will know the truth, and the truth will set you free." John 8:31-32.

> The one who rejects me and does not receive my words has a judge; the word that I have spoken will judge him on the last day. John 12:48.

If I have offended you, please understand I did it unintentionally. If God's word has offended you, be prepared to give an account to him.

> For the word of the cross is folly to those who are perishing, but to us who are being saved it is the power of God. For it is written, "I will destroy the wisdom of the wise, and the discernment of the discerning I will

thwart." 1 Corinthians 1:18-19.

If the words of Christ have pricked your heart, please do not delay, but respond today!

> *Look carefully then how you walk, not as unwise but as wise, making the best use of the time, because the days are evil. Therefore do not be foolish, but understand what the will of the Lord is.* Ephesians 5:15-17.

> *And now why do you wait? Rise and be baptized and wash away your sins, calling on his name.* Acts 22:16.

The next portion of this writing has been provided for you to have a detailed look at some of the Scriptures that have convinced me and others to become true Christians. If you see that the truth is not taught from the Scriptures, please contact me as soon as possible in order to correct me. Only the truth will set us free, not debates, opinion, or speculation. God bless you in the study of his word.

Overview of Studies

Introduction

I highly recommend that you follow the studies in this final chapter with an open Bible. Studying the following subjects has changed my life for eternity. If you allow God's word to penetrate your heart, your own study will change your life, too. Take the time to find these Scriptures in your own Bible, and you will understand the transforming power of God's word.

> *Therefore put away all filthiness and rampant wickedness and receive with meekness the implanted word, which is able to save your souls. But be doers of the word, and not hearers only, deceiving yourselves.* James 1:21-22.

> *For the word of God is living and active, sharper than any two-edged sword, piercing to the division of soul and of spirit, of joints and of marrow, and discerning the thoughts and intentions of the heart.* Hebrews 4:12.

True Belief

It would be hard to find a person who claimed to be a Christian, who also claimed that belief is unimportant. We must, however, address a very important question.

What does it mean to believe in Jesus Christ?

> *For God so loved the world, that he gave his only Son, that whoever believes in him should not perish but have eternal life.* John 3:16.

Jesus said,

> *I told you that you would die in your sins, for unless you believe that I am he you will die in your sins.* John 8:24.

Do you truly believe in Jesus Christ? Do you believe he existed before the world existed (John 17:5)? Do you believe he was born of a virgin through the Holy Spirit (Matthew 1:18), which means he is the Son of God (Luke 1:35)? Do you believe he is Immanuel, "God with us" (Matthew 1:23)? Do you believe he performed the miracles recorded in the New Testament (John 20:30-31)? Do you believe he lived a sinless life (Hebrews 4:14-15)? Do you believe he died for sinners (Romans 5:6-11)? Do you believe he rose on the third day (1 Corinthians 15:1-4)? Do you believe he is reigning at the right hand of God right now (Acts 2:30-35)? Do you believe he is coming back to judge the world (2 Thessalonians 1:6-10)? You must.

Most would agree that referring to Jesus as our *Lord* is important. Although that is true, he says that it's not enough.

> *Not everyone who says to me, "Lord, Lord," will enter the kingdom of heaven, but the one who does the will of my Father who is in heaven. On that day many will say to me, "Lord, Lord, did we not prophesy in your name, and cast out demons in your name, and do many mighty works in your name?" And then will I declare to them, "I never knew you; depart from me, you workers of lawlessness."* Matthew 7:21-23.

In addition to calling Jesus *Lord*, we must do the Father's will, which is found in Scripture. We must obey him from the heart (Romans 6:16-18). If we don't, we won't be set free from the bondage of sin (John 8:31-34). Jesus has become "the source of eternal salvation to all who obey him" (Hebrews 5:8-9).

He will not force his salvation upon you. You must accept the gift he offers on his terms (Hebrews 2:3). He was willing to live as an example for you and die as a sacrifice for you. What will you do for him? Take him for granted? Or will you fall down before him as King of kings and Lord of lords (Revelation 17:14)?

The Church

During his ministry on the earth, Jesus promised his disciples that he would build his church (Matthew 16:18). Of course, he was not referring to a physical building, but to a spiritual building. After Christ fulfilled his promise to establish his church, Peter wrote to the Christians,

> *As you come to him, a living stone rejected by men but in the sight of God chosen and precious, you yourselves like living stones are being built up as a spiritual house, to be a holy priesthood, to offer spiritual sacrifices acceptable to God through Jesus Christ.* 1 Peter 2:4-5.

Each Christian makes up a spiritual stone in Christ's spiritual church.

The Bible refers to Christ's church as his body, of which he is the head (Ephesians 1:22-23). There is only one body (church) of Christ (Ephesians 4:4-6), and Christ is the Savior of that body (Ephesians 5:23). Therefore, for one to be saved, he or she must be a member of Christ's body, his church (1 Corinthians 12:12-13).

In the first century A.D., the early Christians had the tendency to divide. Over and over in the Scriptures, we see Christ and his apostles pleading for unity among the disciples (John 17:20-23; Romans 15:5-7; Philippians 2:1-4). In fact, "dissensions" and "divisions" are listed among the "works of the flesh" that will keep people from inheriting the kingdom of God (Galatians 5:19-21). Paul, in dealing with a specific case of denominationalism, wrote,

> *I appeal to you, brothers, by the name of our Lord Jesus Christ, that all of you agree and that there be no divisions among you, but that you be united in the same mind and the same judgment. For it has been reported to me by Chloe's people that there is quarreling among you, my brothers. What I mean is that each one of you says, "I follow Paul," or "I follow Apollos," or "I follow Cephas," or "I follow Christ." Is Christ divided? Was Paul crucified for you? Or were you baptized in the name of Paul?* 1 Corinthians 1:10-13.

Today, religious division/denominationalism is rampant, though it was condemned in the Scriptures. The phrase, "Join the church of your choice," appeals only to our selfish desires. What about the church of Christ's choice? When we divide into man-made groups, we shake the proverbial fist at God and say, "We see what you want, but we're going to do what we want!"

It is essential to the pure gospel that all those who claim Christ to be in one body of believers. Reject man-made creeds, catechisms, and church manuals, things which the Bible condemns (Deuteronomy 4:2; Proverbs 30:6; Galatians 1:6-12; Revelation 22:18-19), and embrace true, New Testament Christianity. "The Bible only makes Christians only," as the phrase goes. Following "extra rules" makes denominations.

Unfortunately, a couple of brief warnings must be inserted here. Many who feel threatened by the concept of undenominational and predenominational Christianity claim that the church of Christ is a denomination, and a man named Alexander Campbell started it. Very little research needs to be done to disprove this claim. If there is, in fact, a denomination by the name of Church of Christ that was started by some man, I would beg you not to join it, since it cannot be the church that belongs to Christ. No church can be the church that Christ built and be a denomination at the same time. Unlike denominations, the church that Christ purchased with his own blood (Acts 20:28) has no founder but Jesus himself, no rule book but the word of God, and no headquarters on earth.

Though it is unbiblical to refer to the church by manmade names, which are not found in the Bible, a group of people does not have to have the words *church of Christ* on their sign or building in order to be the church of Christ. It would be equally biblical to call them disciples (Acts 11:26), Christians (1 Peter 4:16), the church (Matthew 16:18), the church of God (1 Corinthians 1:2), or the church of Christ (Romans 16:16).

On the other hand, however, if a group refers to itself by one of these designations, that does not automatically make them the biblical church. When looking for Christ's church, "test everything; hold fast what is good" (1 Thessalonians 5:21). Following the Bible only will never make someone a member of a denomination.

Death to Sin

Though Jesus desires all members of all nations to be his disciples (Matthew 28:18-20), he said a couple of things must happen before any person becomes his disciple.

> *Whoever loves father or mother more than me is not worthy of me, and whoever loves son or daughter more than me is not worthy of me. And whoever does not take his cross and follow me is not worthy of me. Whoever finds his life will lose it, and whoever loses his life for my sake will find it.* Matthew 10:37-38.

Before you can decide to follow him, you must make the decision to love him above all else. You must love him more than your stuff, your family, and even yourself. You must be willing to die for him. In fact, before you can even become a disciple, you must do just that (die).

You cannot become a "new creation" in Christ (2 Corinthians 5:17) until you let go of the old person of sin (Romans 6:6). We all spend selfish time in our lives doing exactly as we want, pleasing only ourselves. We must make the mental decision to start pleasing God. That change of heart will lead to a change of action. That concept is the concept of *repentance*.

> *For godly grief produces a repentance that leads to salvation without regret, whereas worldly grief produces death.* 2 Corinthians 7:10.

Recognize that our lives are gifts from God (James 1:17). Therefore, we owe everything to him. Are you willing to give everything back to him? All your possessions? Every breath? Even your relationship with your friends and family? Don't worry; he'll give them back to you, but this time, you must recognize they don't belong to you, but are *entrusted* to you. Will you take care of them?

By definition, breaking God's law is sin (1 John 3:4). Since God is a just God, by default, he must punish sin (Genesis 2:15-17; Romans 6:23). However, God is also a loving God, so he extends grace and forgiveness so that we can be counted as righteous on the basis of our faith (Romans

4; Galatians 3:26-29).

> *In this is love, not that we have loved God but that he loved us and sent his Son to be the propitiation* [atoning sacrifice] *for our sins.* 1 John 4:10.

Therefore, will you die to sin so that you can be made alive in him (Romans 6:1-7)?

> *If your right eye causes you to sin, tear it out and throw it away. For it is better that you lose one of your members than that your whole body be thrown into hell. And if your right hand causes you to sin, cut it off and throw it away. For it is better that you lose one of your members than that your whole body go into hell.* Matthew 5:29-30.

> *For what does it profit a man to gain the whole world and forfeit his life? For what can a man give in return for his life? For whoever is ashamed of me and of my words in this adulterous and sinful generation, of him will the Son of Man also be ashamed when he comes in the glory of his Father with the holy angels.* Mark 8:36-38.

Burial with Christ

Jesus has never asked us to do something that he was not willing to do first. The hardest thing he has asked us to do is to die (to sin). However, it breaks our heart to read the gospel accounts and find out that he died for our sins first. If we would not have been so selfish, he never would have had to die in the first place. Just as he died, we must die to sin through repentance.

> *The times of ignorance God overlooked, but now he commands all people everywhere to repent, because he has fixed a day on which he will judge the world in righteousness by a man whom he has appointed; and of*

this he has given assurance to all by raising him from the dead. Acts 17:30-31.

Once your old person of sin has died, we must do with it what we would normally do with a dead body. We must bury it. The Bible refers to baptism in water as a *burial* (Colossians 2:12). After Jesus' death, he was also buried. Fortunately for us and the rest of the world, he did not stay in the grave, but he was raised on the third day.

For I delivered to you as of first importance what I also received: that Christ died for our sins in accordance with the Scriptures, that he was buried, that he was raised on the third day in accordance with the Scriptures. 1 Corinthians 15:3-4.

And if Christ has not been raised, then our preaching is in vain and your faith is in vain. 1 Corinthians 15:14.

Christ was willing to die, be buried, and be raised. Are you willing to do the same?

What shall we say then? Are we to continue in sin that grace may abound? By no means! How can we who died to sin still live in it? Do you not know that all of us who have been baptized into Christ Jesus were baptized into his death? We were buried therefore with him by baptism into death, in order that, just as Christ was raised from the dead by the glory of the Father, we too might walk in newness of life. For if we have been united with him in a death like his, we shall certainly be united with him in a resurrection like his. Romans 6:1-5.

When I was a baby, a man sprinkled water on my forehead and called it "baptism." However, I hadn't believed or repented yet (Mark 16:16; Acts 2:38). Nor was I "buried with [Christ] in baptism" (Colossians 2:12), since it was just sprinkling.

In the sixth grade, I prayed for Jesus to forgive me and come into my heart, though the Bible never commanded me to do that. In fact, the Bible has never commanded anyone to do that. Instead, it commands people to be "baptized into Christ" (Galatians 3:27), into his body, his church (1 Corinthians 12:12-13), in order to receive "every spiritual blessing," which is "in Christ" (Ephesians 1:3). Some of those spiritual blessings *in Christ* are "eternal life" (Romans 6:23), the "forgiveness of sins" (Colossians 1:13-14), and "salvation" (2 Timothy 2:10).

Do you want to be saved man's way or God's way? Are you willing to biblically "repent and be baptized [...] in the name of Jesus Christ for the forgiveness of your sins" (Acts 2:38)? Since baptism is a burial, you cannot simply be "sprinkled" or have water poured on you. You must be baptized like those in the New Testament, who "went down into the water" and "came up out of the water" (Acts 8:35-39), signifying a burial and resurrection.

> *And Peter said to them, "Repent and be baptized every one of you in the name of Jesus Christ for the forgiveness of your sins, and you will receive the gift of the Holy Spirit. For the promise is for you and for your children and for all who are far off, everyone whom the Lord our God calls to himself." And with many other words he bore witness and continued to exhort them, saying, "Save yourselves from this crooked generation." Acts 2:38-40.*

> *Baptism, which corresponds to this* [those saved in the ark of Noah], *now saves you, not as a removal of dirt from the body but as an appeal to God for a good conscience, through the resurrection of Jesus Christ. 1 Peter 3:21.*

And now why do you wait? Rise and be baptized and wash away your sins, calling on his name. Acts 22:16.

Conclusion

Before reading God's word, I often pray that I am a different person, a better person, after my reading has completed. That prayer is never answered until I'm willing to do my part. Don't take for granted your easy access to God's word. Grab a copy today, whether it's physical or digital. Read it for what it is, and let it change you today.

I am praying that you make the right decision for Christ soon.

Special thanks to Kristen Mosher, "Devin," and Candy Chrisman for proofreading and editing this work.

www.conformedreborntransformed.com

Made in the USA
Charleston, SC
27 July 2015